D0948631

# The Gypsy Scholar

# *The Gypsy Scholar*

## A Writer's Comic Search for a Publisher

### By S. S. HANNA

IOWA STATE UNIVERSITY PRESS, AMES 1987

S. S. Hanna is an Associate Professor of English, Geneva College, Beaver Falls, Pennsylvania

*Drawings by William D. Lee*

© 1987 The Iowa State University Press, Ames, Iowa 50010
All rights reserved
Composed by the Iowa State University Press
Printed in the United States of America

First edition, 1987

**Library of Congress Cataloging-in-Publication Data**
Hanna, S. S., 1943–
  The gypsy scholar.
  1. Authors and publishers. 2. Scholarly publishing. 3. Hanna, S. S., 1943–  . 4. College teachers—United States—Biography. I. Title.
PN155.H27  1987  808'.02  87–2928
**ISBN** 0–8138–1351–4

## THIS LITTLE BOOK IS FOR M. H.

I lit a candle, walked over, stooped and
lit the candle in Sam's tiny hands.
He looked up and smiled.

Walking back, I remembered the time he had
siphoned sunlight with a mirror
and splashed it on your face.

T. S. Eliot spoke for us when he wrote:

"O Light Invisible, we praise Thee!
Too bright for mortal vision.
O Greater Light, we praise Thee for the less;"

# Contents

# Foreword
## PBS, Puffers, Harvard, Termites, and Others

All college professors would love to publish as often as animals mate on the nature programs of PBS television. Few professors do. Most plod along as learned hacks: obscure, undistinguished, but not unhappy. The few who do publish often practice a common ritual: they write books with forewords.

Most books with forewords feature a puffer and a puffee. The puffer, usually a famous person, uses two pages to celebrate the greatness of a given book. The puffee, usually an unknown writer, uses two hundred pages to disprove that lofty estimate.

At first, I considered asking a famous puffer to write this foreword. Then I vetoed that idea and considered pivoting the entire foreword on a rejection letter that I had received from the Harvard University Press. In time, I chucked the Harvard idea and incorporated into the foreword a brief dialogue on writing that I had with a student of mine at Geneva College. The dialogue lasted for several days until one morning I walked up to my third-floor office in Fern Cliffe Hall, a Victorian clapboard structure erected in 1870, read the dialogue out loud, dramatized some phrases with those professorial whistle-grunt combinations, and concluded that the dialogue was as bad as it sounded. I tossed it and glanced at a plastered chimney planted near the center of the L-shaped, book-lined office. I paced the spacious office, stood in the alcoves of its arched windows, looked at the campus below, and decided to write another foreword.

One day "Termites in a Yo-Yo," an unpublished short story of mine that was searching for a publisher, came back with a note that read, "This is excellent, but it doesn't meet our current needs." I instantly thought of sending the rejecting editor another story with a cover letter that read, "The enclosed might meet your current needs. It's mediocre." Given the content and character of this book, I thought of focusing its foreword on these and other related letters.

In time, I vetoed the "Termites" idea and reasoned: "Since excerpts from this book have originally appeared in *Publishers Weekly* and the *Chronicle of Higher Education*, then this book could be 'guilty by association' with these distinguished forums. These forums, in effect, could serve as its puffers. What remains for me to do is say in a few words what this book is about."

Every year, many college professors and writers undertake the often frustrating search for book publishers. Few, however, write about their experiences with a light—and instructive—touch. This book attempts to do just that.

It follows a two-part format. Part one abridges a nonfiction book manuscript that I had circulated to commercial houses, university presses, and literary agents. Part two reproduces and narrates—with a wink at the ironic—the numerous letters that I had sent and received on the manuscript. I abridged the manuscript to give the readers a feel for its contents and an opportunity "to play editor" with it. Indeed, the readers might enjoy comparing their estimates with those of established editors at various presses.

If this little book works, the readers should learn about a gypsy scholar teaching English, coaching football, and working at the writer's craft. If it works well, the readers should be entertained by a self-deprecating comic style. If it works extremely well, the readers should learn, smile, and smuggle away some clues on how to get their book-length manuscripts professionally published.

One final—but crucial—note: I deeply respect the academic institutions where I had taught and coached and the book publishers with whom I had corresponded. I say this because the word "comic" in the book's subtitle might unwittingly blur that respect, a respect that I hope remains clear and strong throughout *The Gypsy Scholar*.

# PART ONE
# THE GYPSY SCHOLAR

## CHAPTER ONE

# Indiana:
## Search for That First Job

In the early seventies when I completed a Ph.D. in literature at Indiana University, herds of Ph.D.s roamed jobless
throughout the land. I joined them at their favorite pas-
time: soliciting "no vacancy . . . open file" type letters. I
wrote 295 individually typed letters and sent them, along
with my curriculum vita, to academic deans of small colleges and department heads at large universities. Most replies were typed, cold, and formal. I ignored them. One reply, however, infuriated me.

   That reply came from an old friend, a young man who
in the midsixties grew a beard, strummed a guitar, and
whined about his identity crisis; at times, he grabbed a
placard and demonstrated with the devoted members of the
Dow Chemical greeting committee. As a graduate student,
he worked as a teaching assistant in English and completed
his doctoral dissertation several semesters before I began
mine. When he graduated, the job market for Ph.D.s was so
good that he located a position that led to a chairmanship
of a tiny department in an underdeveloped state university
that shall remain nameless.

   To my friend I wrote a cordial and rather personal letter.

For a reply I received a stenciled sheet with the appropriate boxes checked. The chairman's name appeared on the mimeographed sheet in a sketchy, abrupt manner. I reacted to his cold and terribly impersonal reply, and I did so—not impulsively, but in a calculated and crafty manner.

Specifically, I wrote the dean of the graduate school at Indiana University, the school that we had attended, and inquired about a teaching position. What I really wanted, however, was not a position (I realized before I wrote how hopeless that was) but a copy of the dean's stationery. When the dean replied, I had in my hands a negative letter. But it was more than that. It was a potentially explosive grenade with a string only a United States mailman could pull.

One evening I drafted a letter and addressed it to the chairman, using his full name, title, and position. The letter stated:

Dear Dr. However: [Not his real name]

It gives me great pain to inform you that by order of the Board of Trustees I am now engaged in the process of recalling many of the Ph.D.s that have been granted by this University during the last decade.

As you know from a quick glance at *Time, Newsweek,* the *Chronicle of Higher Education* or some of the other forums dealing with education, the job market of this country is glutted with Ph.D.s. This is due to the fact that way back in the sixties, many students dodged the very unfortunate Vietnam conflict by attending graduate school. It is also due to the fact that our graduate schools—and on these very charges we are culpable—eased up on the traditional language requirements and the measure of excellence in both the preliminary examinations and the scholarly dissertation.

These urgent matters have recently been brought to our attention by the various foundations studying higher education. In keeping with their cogent and highly incisive recommendations—soon to be made public—we are recalling a rather substantial number of our Ph.D.s. Your Ph.D., I am very sorry to say, has been nominated as one of those to be recalled this month.

I would, therefore, request you to return to my office by registered mail the original copy of your degree. If you have any questions, kindly address them—in writing please—to me, and I shall be happy to see to it that you receive a prompt reply.

The original copy of this letter is with the president of the University, who is closely observing this rather sensitive operation. I am forwarding to you, under separate cover, the copies of your dissertation that have been deposited with this University. I trust you will bear with us during this difficult period of transition.

I look forward to hearing from you at your earliest convenience. With best wishes, I remain

Sincerely yours,

DONALD A. JONES III

Graduate School, Dean

c.c. University Placement Bureau
    Current Employer

P.S. The Board of Trustees' decision in your case was unanimous. They also voted, unanimously once again, to allow you to keep your Ph.D. regalia. Their reasons are articulated in a notarized statement that is available on request.


I typed the letter and then pasted it on the dean's letter to me, the letter that claimed he had no teaching vacancies. Of course, I positioned the letter so that the impressive stationery, the names of the dean and the graduate school, the emblem and the Latin motto of the university—all appeared in their utmost grandeur. I then headed to a Xerox machine and copied the mock-up three times on quality paper. That done, I rushed to the post office, registered one copy of the letter and mailed it special delivery to my old friend. Two days later, I called and heard him say, "We just sat down to eat breakfast when the mailman delivered this letter—"

"The who?" I interrupted.

"The mailman," came the reply.

"The person-person we say these days," I suggested and chuckled ever so slightly. My friend refused to laugh. Instead, he spoke sadly and touchingly of the tragic news that had just arrived, and he wondered whether I had received similar news.

"Yes," I claimed. Then I baited the chairman, "Are they serious or is this a stunt or what?" I tried to sound concerned and anxious. In the background I overheard the anguish of his wife who sounded terribly disturbed, baffled, angry—and breakfastless, perhaps.

Moments before I explained the stunt to my friend, I overheard his wife groan, "I told you, honey, you should have taken an Ed.D."

Unlike my friend's cold and impersonal reply, I received one that was warm and personal. It was a response to an unusual letter that I had written to Dr. Thomas C. Mendenhall, president of Smith College in Northampton, Massachusetts. My letter said:

Dear Dr. Mendenhall,

If I am unable to locate a teaching position in literature for the next year, I expect to be washing dishes. In this letter, I wish to assess my background and interests which might lead you to hire me to your staff at Smith College or to recommend me to the dishwashing profession. Enclosed is my vita.

My general academic record is quite impressive. It consists of many courses (ninety semester hours at the graduate level), excellent grades (3.8 on the 4.0 scale), and several publications in leading journals and magazines. One of the publications has been translated into French by Professor Jean Lecerf of the Sorbonne and has appeared in *Orient*, a Sorbonne-based periodical.

I am twenty-six, and I would love to commence my teaching career. During my graduate years, I held a National Defense Fellowship on two different occasions and a University Fellowship; moreover, I received an assistantship and a research grant. To sum up: I am good and

I can do more good in the teaching profession than in the world of liquid Joy.
Please hire me.

Sincerely,

S. S. HANNA

P.S. I will accept a part-time appointment—anything. My complete dossier, file number 31692, is with the Indiana University Bureau of Educational Placement, School of Education, Bloomington, Indiana. 47401.

Dr. Mendenhall wrote his reply in a felt pen and dated it in the British style—first the day, then the month. He addressed the envelope, sealed it, and licked the stamp. I thought of incorporating his reply into an allegorical piece on job hunting in the early seventies. His reply in full stated:

Dear S. S. Hanna,
Though I have nothing to offer or suggest, I somehow cannot let your plea for a teaching position go unanswered! There is nothing at Smith and I know of nothing around us in the Valley. I am sure you have tried the usual places; so the most you can do is keep trying, for your knowledge and interests will surely find a taker somewhere.
So don't despair, and try cooking rather than dishwashing. The need is greater, and the pay better.
With best wishes,

T. C. MENDENHALL

I didn't despair, for I landed a job flipping—cooking—hamburgers and washing dishes at a local restaurant. Most of the summer I remained without a teaching position; I found myself strapped to the routine of rocking in my favorite chair, reading "Little" and literary magazines, caring for my pure mutt Prufrock, recording my thoughts in a diary, and often wondering how many other Ph.D.s throughout the land shared my predicament. I wondered about my fate and the fate of my immediate peers at Indiana University. Herds of jobless Ph.D.s in America document a crisis. In attempting to understand, prod, resolve, indeed humor my role in that crisis, I returned to my diary and recorded my reactions to the replies elicited by my query letters. Here are several sample entries:

Tues. 2/Only twenty-two letters arrived this morning, all harping on the same old theme: sorry no vacancy, but we're happy to place your letter in an open file. In an age scrambling for Ph.D. dissertation topics, the nature of these rejection letters and their impact on the lives of young Ph.D.s might be a topic worth researching.

. . . . .

Fri. 5/To one of those exclusive women's colleges that is now striving for a balance between debutantes and dudesses, I wrote the following after perusing their catalogue, "As a young man of twenty-six, I feel I could participate in [quoting their catalogue] 'that exciting interaction that goes on between faculty and students at the College.'" In his reply, the academic dean wrote a classic no-vacancy, open-file type letter and then proceeded to thank me for my "kind words relating to [quoting my letter that quoted the catalogue] 'that exciting . . . .'" My one word poem [yeast] has been out with the *Paris Review* for a while now, and I'm thinking of placing a courtesy call to inquire about its status.

. . . . .

Mon. 8/College athletes who read, write, and do math at fifth-grade level or below and who are recruited on "scholarships"—really "jockships"—to play football or basketball at major universities are in the news again. Nobody seems to know what to do with those athletes, but I do know what should be done to the universities who recruit them: these universities should be required to surrender their memberships in the Phi Beta Kappa society, for no Phi Beta Kappa university should be allowed to admit such proven underachievers. Vietnam is also in the news again. Today's negative letters led me to wonder just how many Ph.D.s may be traced to the fear of the rice paddies of Vietnam; this sounds like another good dissertation topic for a struggling Ph.D.-to-be. I hope this Ph.D. dissertation topic stuff is a stage that all fresh Ph.D.s go through, kind of like teething for a baby. This evening I read more engaging accounts dealing with T. S. Eliot's conversion to Christianity; indeed, Eliot's entire spiritual pilgrimage haunts me in a pleasantly disturbing way. Why did Eliot, at the height of his literary career, commit his life to Christ? I often ask this, as I continue to row—and row—back.

. . . . .

Thur. 11/Twenty-four replies in today's mail, fourteen of which are mimeographed. I've developed a new method to detect whether the letters are mimeographed or not, and now it's getting to the point where I enjoy its application. Holding the letter up against the light is the old, somewhat unreliable, method. My approach, besides being fresh and new and original, is certainly foolproof. It goes like this: I fondle the back of the letter. If it is smooth, very, very smooth, then I conclude that it is mimeographed or xeroxed. If it is somewhat coarse, then it is freshly typed. What really irks me are those letters that tell me, via the use of a stencil, how terribly impressed they are with my credentials. But they don't stop there. They go on and submit all those apologies for having no vacancies and quickly assure me of placing my letter in an open file. A closed file would be a far more hopeful promise, for that might mean the letters are being tucked away someplace in a metal cabinet. The aroma of sizzling bacon whips one into submission; rejection letters do too, but I don't enjoy their strokes. "And the Brook Dried Up" engaged my attention today; it's powerful, moving, poignant.

. . . . .

Fri. 12/After receiving today's twenty-four rejections I decided that the Turks of Istanbul might put a man on the moon before I land a teaching position. Today I finished reading the *Confessions* of St. Augustine. Professor David _____ was admitted to the Bloomington hospital for a hernia operation. (He must have been doing some heavy thinking.) This evening I went to see him.

. . . . .

Mon. 15/In one of my letters, typed no doubt when I was tired and sluggish, I noted: "Besides my extensive curse work, the highlights of my record are my publications, honors, and experience." Picking on this, one careful and indeed Christian dean wrote: "It helps to have extensive 'course work' instead of 'curse work,' but in any event, we don't have a vacancy for someone with your background and experience, and we do not anticipate one to develop in the foreseeable future." I had a hot cup of brown water (why he insists on calling it coffee beats me) at Jack's almost Victorian Mobile home; Jack plans to kiss the Ph.D. "goodbye" and peck a "hello" on an M.B.A.

. . . . .

Fri. 19/Sam took a copy of his dissertation and went for an interview today. This merely strengthens my belief in miracles. I hope he gets the job. He is one of three Ph.D.s that the little college plans to interview. He seems to think that the job will go to the candidate who has the biggest troop of kids to support. He's paying his way there and back, though he expects to be fed at the college's cafeteria. Two jobless Ph.D.s and I ate a vegetarian dinner at Paul's pad. The food was fair to partly tasty; the dinner gave me an idea for a poem: compare a jobless vegetarian with a meatless dish.

. . . . .

Tues. 23/Well, well. A small college in Ohio asks me (via a rubber stamp on the rejection letter): "Do You Have the College in Your Will?" Here I am, desperate and despairing, poor, penniless, broke, in quest of a full-time, a half-time, a part-time teaching position. Any position. Today, I sent out for rejection two stories of mine entitled, "Cockroache in the Sculptured Hairdo" and "Don't Even Think of Parking Here." I began a solicited book review of translated poems with this sentence: "Mother tongues father the best poetry." I wonder if it'll survive the editor's pen at *Books Abroad*. Tonight I cooked aquatic question marks.

. . . . .

Thurs. 25/In today's replies, one chairperson returned my curriculum vita and said: "Permit me, please, to put your letter in an open file." This fellow gave it away. What kind of an open file is it that has a cover letter to a vita and not the vita itself? I called my mother on her sixty-first birthday and perplexed her when I told her that—even after ten years of college and graduate school and a Ph.D.—I still didn't have a college teaching job. My two brothers-in-law, she reminded me, had excellent jobs, and my dad, a clerk in a factory, was working overtime. Today I worked on a confessional poem that compares a young writer coveting the Christian temperament of his literary hero to a sensitive man coveting the elegant antiques of a poor and lonely widow.

. . . . .

Sat. 27/Among today's set of rejections, a most refreshing letter came from a small college in Maine. In his reply to my inquiry, the dean congratulated me on my courage to take on the "rigor of Maine's winter" and froze my vita and its cover letter in an open file. Tonight I finished Elisabeth Elliot's *Through Gates of Splendor.* A powerful book.

. . . . .

Tues. 2/Thirty-three no-vacancy, open-file letters arrived today. Thirty-three. They crucified our Lord and Savior at that age, and in pain he spoke, "Father, forgive them for they know not what they do." My earnest prayer remains: "Lord I believe; help thou mine unbelief."

. . . . .

Fri. 5/In today's pile of letters, a glittering gem, quarried at a small college in Nebraska, read, "Sorry, we have been forced to close down the college. If we reopen and need you, we'll call you." That college reminds me of poor Bob. Kathy claims to be allergic to him, and she sees divorce as the only cure. Today, I continued work on a short story that develops the theme: poor people are generous. I also added two metaphors to the idea file of "The Muttering Retreats," a long poem that I plan to write once I get a large block of time. The poem's central theme has been a pervasive part of my life—with different levels of intensity—since childhood. The theme: Christ sculptures in us the pain to endure.

. . . . .

Tues. 9/Hard to believe. This evening while browsing in the library, I came across a most relevant piece of research. It is a doctoral dissertation done right here at Indiana University. The dissertation deals with, of all topics, letters of recommendation, and it is entitled, shrewdly enough, "An Analysis of Letters of Recommendation." It was accepted in 1961—all eighty-eight pages of it. ("Brevity is the soul of wit.") Now really. In 1961 the study might have been an important breakthrough. Perhaps it was a major contribution to scholarship of that decade, the sixties, a decade when many college students needed a good scrutiny. It might have pushed the bounds of knowledge; after all, it was a doctoral dissertation. (The only way a person could push the bounds of knowledge with my dissertation would be to place it on a library cart and shove the cart around.) In any event, what this decade needs is not a survey, not an analysis, not an introduction to, but a systematic study of those no-vacancy, open-file letters. If some aspiring doctoral student here or elsewhere decides to take on this challenge, I shall have for his or her examination the world's largest archives.

. . . . .

Fri. 12/At last a nice and fat envelope came in today's batch. I did not open it right away; I set it aside, thinking that it might be an application for a position. I poured a cup of coffee, relaxed on my rocker, and then gently opened the envelope. The cover letter advised me that "no vacancy exists and none is anticipated in the near future." The enclosed material consisted of a neatly designed Catholic pamphlet that opened with these words: "IF YOU DIE TODAY, DO YOU KNOW IF YOU'LL GO TO HEAVEN?" Since I had not planned on dying today, I delivered the pamphlet to Keane, a Catholic friend who is also desperately searching for a teaching position. "Maybe you can pray your way to a job," I told Keane, only to hear him reply, "Even that does not seem to work these days." After a slight pause, Keane delivered a little sermon in which he shared with me God's formula for answering prayer. "God answers prayer in four ways," he began, then he elaborated, "One, God might say, 'No, I love you too much.' Two, God might say, 'Wait a while, you'll be surprised.' Three, God might say, 'Yes, by all means, thought you'd never ask, and here's more.' Four, God might say—and this is the answer that I keep getting for my ceaseless supplications for a college teaching position—'Son, you've got to be kidding.' And about this tract," Keane added, as he handed it back to me, "you don't need it. Give it to a bad surgeon and urge him to pass it on to one of his patients, preferably a Ph.D. with a job." As I write this, Prufrock is sprawled near my feet, scratching his chest, doing his imitation of a hippie playing the guitar.

. . . . .

Sun. 14/I'm back to reading the writings of Jonathan Edwards, the Puritan divine who was the subject of my Senior Thesis in college. And I've also been enjoying the wisdom of Thomas à Kempis's *Imitation of Christ*. This evening, the early editors (they're still alive) of *Cantaloupe* came up; we met and congratulated ourselves on publishing each other in our "Little" magazine. They left calling it "the late *Cantaloupe*." It's the 14th of June, and there's still no job in sight.

. . . . .

Besides recording those thoughts in the diary that I came to call "The Love Song of a Jobless Scholar," I enjoyed an occasional meal with my graduate school buddies, the jobless members of the footnote brigade. None of us expected to be wined and dined or beered and barbecued by a college or university. All of us, however, longed to be proven wrong. Keane hoped that God would foresake His "you've got to be kidding" trend. I hoped to thank God one day from a cabin in heaven—no smoking section. I hoped, prayed, waited. And waited. Finally that job interview day did arrive.

It was late in July when I flew to a town in Oklahoma, sat for an interview at a small (1600 students) liberal arts institution, and flew back to Bloomington as an assistant professor of English at Oklahoma Baptist University (founded in 1910). As it turned out, I was watered and dined by the good folks in Oklahoma at Shawnee's Mandarin Garden, an overdecorated Chinese restaurant in the land of the baptized Indians where the bumper stickers read HONK IF YOU

LOVE JESUS and/or AMERICA LOVE IT OR GIVE IT BACK, and where the license plates say OKLAHOMA IS OK. During my two-day interview at OBU, I learned a great deal about the school from an engaging and handsome Ph.D. from the University of Chicago, an assistant professor of history who guided me on an extensive tour of the spacious campus. The historian was extremely pleased with OBU's academic quality and especially with the quality of its young faculty, most of whom had Ph.D.s from the country's leading universities. He pointed out that OBU had no graduate programs, but it was called a university because of its two-school structure: The College of Liberal Arts and the School of Music. He mentioned that many OBU graduates had excelled in such fields as medicine, religion, music, law, and education. He listed the names of recent graduates who were attending some first-rate graduate schools; he chuckled when he said that the "Shawnee resident who went the farthest became an astronaut, one of the original seven." He praised the school's library facilities and made particular reference to its "highly efficient" interlibrary-loan system. The historian also noted that "OBU, unlike many small church-related colleges, permits its students and faculty to smoke on campus, but like most such colleges, OBU prohibits its students from drinking and dancing. Faculty members," he added, "are free to drink and dance in the privacy of their own homes, but not in restaurants or bars."

At coffee in the Student Union, the Chicago scholar mentioned with pride OBU's film series and its visiting lecturers' programs. Among those scheduled to speak on campus were poet John Ciardi, ABC's science reporter Jules Bergman, Senator Edmund Muskie of Maine, author Milton Viorst, NBC correspondent Robert Goralski, native son astronaut Gordon Cooper, and Black leader Julian Bond. "And regarding academic freedom," he said, "you'll get all that one gets at a state university and—if you stop and think about it—you'll probably get more here, for here we are free to preach Christ if we wish, we may integrate our faith with our discipline. We have a sharp academic dean who sees to it that our academic freedom remains strong and healthy."

The historian had failed to say a thing about the salary scale. After I had left him and headed to the dean's office for a final visit, the dean said as he handed me a contract with salary figures, "Now let's talk turkey." I looked at the figures and said to myself, "No wonder the historian said nothing about the salary scale; these figures look more like a Cornish hen to me." And the historian had also failed to say a thing about the campus; he left it for me to judge the campus's beauty or lack of it. On the plane ride back to Bloomington, I remembered a well-groomed oval with neatly trimmed evergreens, lush grass, and lamppost-lined walks; I also remembered a number of red-brick, neo-Georgian, colonial-style buildings; and I remembered all sorts of broad stairs and wide, round, and high pillars that gave the buildings an imposing and majestic look. I remembered those white, magnificent, ever so graceful columns of Shawnee Hall, for they appeared to give the hall an expansive, mystical feel as if it were a lyceum in the Home of the Redman. To me, the OBU campus appeared attractive indeed, and I looked forward to working there.

In Bloomington it took me nearly a week to pack all my materials and a day to sell most of my junk at a yard sale. I spent the better part of a Monday stacking my belongings in the back of a U Haul that I had hitched to my station wagon. The last day in Bloomington was a sad one; I said farewell to my jobless buddies, tenured professors, and favorite places. The forthcoming football season in Bloomington promised to be typically poor; I didn't expect to miss it. I knew that I would miss the dudes of winter: the basketball season. Bobby Knight's Hoosiers had enough of a reputation that I expected to see them on national television on several occasions. The saddest part of my departure from Bloomington came when I took Prufrock and his dog food to a professor who had agreed to offer the dog a new home. I resisted the temptation to explain to Prufrock what it meant for a Ph.D. to have a job. I felt he must have understood, intuitively.

While driving out of Bloomington on a muggy morning in August, I began to listen to my favorite programs on Public Radio. That morning, the international news was particularly depressing: it detailed another brutal and nauseating act in Soviet atrocities, it pointed to bloody riots in a Third World country, it graphed in vivid language a famine in Africa, to mention a few of the items. The newscasts—on stations that would fade and on stations that would emerge—amplified these stories and added others, just as horrible or even more so.

As I drove on and on, I looked back at the years in Bloomington when the chores and routines of a given day had often prevented me from brooding on the news, however revolting it appeared. I suddenly found myself without the luxury of my daily routines; I was imprisoned in a car for miles on end, so the frequent newscasts stirred my sensitivity, forcing me to assess and probe, to meditate and moan, to listen and muse. At one instance, I remembered several lines from a poem that I had written; the lines lingered with me like a migraine, and I recited them outloud many times. For miles, I found myself brooding on the turmoil in these lines:

> We watch them clip
> the breasts of cows
> and fill the pots
> with blood and milk

From a restaurant on the outskirts of Oklahoma, I telephoned my mother in Milwaukee and told her about my eight-thousand-dollar job as an assistant professor at OBU, a job that she felt paid "peanuts" when compared to the pay of my two brothers-in-law, one of whom was a banker and the other an engineer. "And remember," she said, "both didn't go to college for ten years."

As I drove on to Shawnee, I picked up on Public Radio Woodie Guthrie singing:

> Way down yonder on the Indian nation
> Ride my pony on the reservation
> Oklahoma hills where I was born . . .

## CHAPTER TWO

# Oklahoma:
# A Young Professor,
# a "Little" Magazine

Two weeks before registration for the fall semester, I drove into Shawnee with a U Haul still attached to my rusty but reliable station wagon. They were packed with books, art work, clothes, a television, a rocker, a dresser, a stereo, records, magazines, football mementos, a bed, a desk, an oak library table, an old church pew, and assorted items bought at Hoosier auctions. The drive from Indiana had been long and dull. I headed to the Cinderella Motel of interview days, shaved, showered, and swam; at dinner, I read all the material that I could locate dealing with Shawnee city of Pottawatomie County of central Oklahoma. I had a slight problem falling asleep, so I pulled out of my briefcase a reprint of a scholarly article of mine that had arrived in the mail during my last day in Bloomington; I began to read it, only to sleep with the quickness and certitude induced by an anesthesiologist's needle.

The next day I parked the U-Haul in front of the impressive, pillar-braced administration building and went to see the kind and helpful academic dean about possible leads on housing. University housing was reserved for married faculty with children. Unattached faculty members looked for flats in town. The dean drove me to three apartment complexes, new and neat and cheap in appearance, with all the trappings of the lower class on the rise: shag rug, communal swimming pool, dangling lamps with glass that had tumors, large reproductions of famous paintings. When we toured the third apartment complex, I mustered enough courage and impatience and honesty to say to the dean, "To tell you the truth, these modern places do not appeal to me at all."

"I'll show you another available place where one of our married students lived, but I doubt if you'd like it."

We drove to the university and parked the car on the edge of the oval in front of the music building. We walked across Kickapoo and entered the Campus Drugs. There, we obtained the key, exited through the back door, and climbed the steps leading to what instantly struck me as a marvelous flat—spacious and dirty, with a marble fireplace.

"I'll take this," I said impulsively, trusting my impulse.

"Are you sure?" the dean asked, then added, "This place needs a lot of work, but then it's relatively inexpensive."

"How much is this place?"

"This is eighty-five dollars with all bills paid by the owner, but the other places that I had shown you run in the two-hundred dollars, and you have to pay the bills."

"Yeah," I said, "I'll sure take this place."

"But this place is dirty."

"I'll clean it."

"Are you sure you want this?"

"Yes, I'm sure, sure, sure."

"This place has so much character," the dean said.

"Yep," I agreed as my eyes scanned the walls, floors, doors, ceiling, and woodwork; with my hands in the side pockets of my pants, I slowly paced the place, nodding, popping my eyebrows, stretching my neck muscles, inwardly smiling. "Yes, sir," I said, "this place sure has character!"

"And it has potential too," the dean added.

"Yeah, lots of potential."

"That it does."

"I can make one of these rooms into my study, the other into a bedroom, and I'll still have a living room, a dining

room, a bath. Yeah, this place is great, just great."
"OK," the dean said, "I'll talk to the owner, who always cooperates with us, and I'll get you squared away. Do you have enough furniture to fill this place?"
"I've got some, and I'll go to auctions and buy some more. That's the least of my problems. Let me stay here and look around for a while," I told the dean.

He rambled down the steps, appearing awkwardly pleased. After he formalized the deal with the owner of the Campus Drugs, he returned and instructed me to pay the owner $85 at the beginning of each month and "go down and sign a few papers as soon as possible. If you clean the place yourself," the dean continued, "you won't have to pay rent for these last remaining days in August." Before leaving, he informed me of his plans to ask the Buildings and Grounds division of the university to send two young men to help me unload the U Haul.

With all the stuff in the living room, I thanked the departing young men and walked around the apartment. I opened the lone kitchen cabinet, the size of a fat midget's coffin, and observed several cockroaches on maneuvers. I closed the cabinet and walked into a bedroom; there, I spotted more cockroaches. Immediately, I dubbed the place Roach Hall and continued my casual tour. I walked into the small room that I had planned to use for a study and stood in place for a moment or two; my thoughts wandered and envisioned an obscure Ph.D. candidate somewhere doing research on cockroaches: studying, sorting, and classifying them. I saw the budding scholar assessing his data, formulating trends and types, amassing figures, facts, and footnotes; and I also saw him assigning a "suicidal" classification to those cockroaches that refused to align themselves with the data; I hoped most of my cockroaches would fall into this classification. (The uses of those pointed cowboy boots lit up my mind like a Joycean epiphany). I refused to despair. Shawnee's red-brick Cedar Terrace apartments, with their images of plastic, were no match for the second floor walk-up flat of the Campus Drugs overlooking the Grubsteak, a student hangout.

Instead of despairing, I headed down to a grocery store to

buy detergent, sponges, pails, cockroach killer, and air freshener. The walls of the place were so dirty, I reasoned, that they really needed a paint job. But that would have to wait for another semester. For now, I felt, my posters and art work in cahoots with some dim lights would have to do.

At a tiny grocery store with faded bread advertisements that had once been painted on the brick walls, I collected the needed items and placed them on a counter. Then I stood and admired the cash register, with its gilded paint peeling and flaking, revealing its age that must have dated back to the Dust Bowl days of Oklahoma. A green and white poster hugged the cash register. The poster proclaimed, "SHOPPERS SAVE."

"Shoppers save where?" I smiled and kidded the Indian whose head barely peeked above the cash register.

"At the Federal National Bank, but if you ask me on 'what' items they save, then I'll tell you on just about every item in here." As he rang up my items, I reached over and picked a religious tract from the pile beside the cash register. The cover of the tract asked, "Whose Religion Saves?" It listed Catholics, Methodists, Presbyterians, Episcopalians, and Baptists. When I noted that the labels referred to denominations and not religions, the Indian gently insisted that I read the tract and follow its five-step plan. "You sound like a double-negative English teacher," he added, stroking that remark with a big smile.

"Well, you got that right," I said, "I'm going to be teaching English at OBU."

"Welcome to Shawnee," the Indian said, "OBU is a great school; two of my sons graduated from there and they've got excellent jobs now."

Later that day, I returned to buy some light bulbs from the Indian's grocery store. While there, I listened to him talk at length. He was a jovial Kickapoo who spoke with fondness and nostalgia about the Kickapoo Nation, its proud warrior heritage cast against the backdrop of the Indian diaspora. He also talked about his life as I marveled at the tracks and islands of skin fossiled in his round burgundy face. I learned that he was a disabled World War II veteran who had fought in the Battle of the Bulge. "And I fought like all Kickapoos," he exclaimed, "with great pride and honor and courage, for Kickapoos are grand warriors with an amazing degree of ethnic purity."

As I was leaving the store that afternoon, the Kickapoo directed me to a large lumber yard run, as he put it, "by a wonderful Kickapoo Injeian." There, I bought bricks and boards to be used in setting up my study in Roach Hall. In a day or two, speakers and books, maps and rugs, posters and paintings, records, sculptures, poignant photographs and eclectic furnishings, coffee mugs, literary tabloid covers, a T. S. Eliot poster, a huge painting of a crucifixion scene fraught with tranquility and pain—all neatly cluttered my walk-up flat, giving it that old graduate student touch. 2311 North Kickapoo in Shawnee, Oklahoma, might have passed for an apartment in the student ghettos of Madison or Bloomington, Norman or New Haven, Ames or Cambridge, even though the cat and the plants were still missing.

Two days before traveling to Shawnee for the job interview, I had cut my hair and trimmed by mustache. Several weeks later, my hair—or halo, as I should really say—had grown long again. To keep a proper professorial appearance, I felt it prudent to cut my hair and keep it short and neat. Accordingly, I went to a Shawnee barbershop and watched a certain Sam [not his real name] take charge of my head.

Sam was in his seventies at least, and his bifocals had crusts of glass. A slight limp punctuated his walk. He started to cut my hair and to sprinkle me with spit and wisdom while doing it. "It's not a disgrace to be poor," Sam said while commenting on the nation's economic situation, "it's just an inconvenience." The radio blurted a news report on inflation; the report led Sam to inform me that "Years ago, I used to say, 'The sweat of today is the sweet juice of tomorrow.' But now with all this inflation stuff," (he flipped off the clippers in order to make sure that I heard his booming voice) "I say, 'The sweat of today is the sweet sorrow of tomorrow.'"

In time, Sam's aphoristic lectures led him to attack people whose ideas freeze into dogma. "Some people are so dogmatic," he said, "that if they tell you that the sky is green, you shouldn't argue with them; what you should say is, 'Oh, yes, yes, you're so right, so very right, as a matter of fact I see grass up there.'" Sam continued speaking as he turned the barber's chair so that my head faced the mirror at which point I saw my head and reflections of passing cars and trucks. The shifting-grinding gears of one truck led Sam to say, "Those truck drivers, they're the Knights of the Road who keep on truckin' to the tunes of Johnny Cash and Loretta Lynn and Merle Haggard."

As he began to crop the hair around my ears, he advised me, "Never claim to be bald."

"I never do," I told Sam.

"You never what?" he snapped.

"You heard me right," I said.

"But I see you *right* here in front of me," he said, poking my head.

"You see, I simply say that I part my hair in a circle."

He laughed and said, "It looks more like a horseshoe to me." After a brief pause, he added, "You know what we barbers say about baldness, 'The good Lord created so many perfect heads, the rest he covered with hair.' You see, this is a defense from a religious perspective." As an afterthought he reminded me, "Now you'll still be bald, but at least you'd have a good defense for it." When he finished cutting my hair, he tapped my pate with his index finger, leaned back to admire my halo, then asked, "Now, how's that for a half-decent job?"

Following the haircut, I went to Shawnee Hall to arrange my office and see what items remained there after the previous instructor left and the other professors played "trading post" by exchanging chairs, tables, shelves, file cabinets. I was surprised and pleased to note the splendid furniture in the clean and spacious office. Moments later, I felt the need to wash my neck of hair splinters, so I went downstairs to the men's room, only to find myself in the john, sitting with a writing pad in front of me much as a journalist does in a White House news conference. I scribbled away, copying several of the thoughts that decorated the walls and door of that compartment. One person wrote, "I was in Norman when Notre Dame made big men cry"; below that, someone added, "I hate ND." (In 1957, Notre Dame's football squad snapped Oklahoma's forty-seven game winning streak.) Another person wrote, "My biology professor has more degrees than a thermometer." Next to that, someone added, "Well, that makes him a pretty hot doctor." A third person corrected that by writing, "You mean a Ph.D."

The Ph.D. graffiti reminded me of an autobiographic essay that I had started to write while in Bloomington entitled "Farewell to Footnotes." I had hoped the essay would lead me away from writing dissertation-type criticism and launch me on a career as a neglected minor poet or an obscure writer of comic prose—be it fiction or nonfiction.

My first Monday in Shawnee, we had a long—a very long, a day long—faculty meeting. Along with other new faculty members, I was introduced at that meeting. Throughout the meeting, I listened, doodled, mated words, collided images with figurative language; I even wrote an epitaph for my Epitaph Factory Series. The epitaph addressed an artist-friend back in Bloomington:

> She lived
> an artist, died a connoisseur of
> negative spaces

During a break in the afternoon session, I balanced a coffee cup in my right hand and stood on the periphery of a small group of scholars and listened to a playful dispute on the qualifications needed to teach the Unified Studies course in the Humanities, one of the required core courses in a solid, demanding, and well-integrated liberal arts curriculum. I remember one professor who argued for "a specialist in something, a scholar who doesn't mind being a generalist"; another professor suggested that "a generalist by training and inclination is what the Humanities course needs"; a third injected humor into the dispute by calling for "a specialist in generalities." That bit of humor, coupled with occasional swipes at "jocks in culture classes," incited one of the coaches—the university's court jester, as I later learned. The coach stepped forward and said, "When our students come and tell us that they just chose to major in quote-unquote phys. ed., that, my dear friends and colleagues, is their last choice. But still," he continued, "we do have a sense of athletics—aesthetics—around the gym. I personally enjoy looking at the Mona Lisa every once in a while, not every day, but every once in a while; and on occasions, we do spin a metaphor here and there. For example, we don't say that an awkward basketball player is terribly uncoordinated; we say, instead, he's as coordinated as a pig on ice. End of quotation."

Several days after that first faculty meeting, I walked into the faculty lounge, prepared a cup of coffee, sat on a lounge chair and began to listen to the conversation in progress. Before long, one faculty member turned to me and said, "Dr. Hanna, you just finished looking for a job, how's the market these days?"

"Tight, extremely tight," I replied.

"Just how tight is extremely tight?" He asked.

"Well, I'll be specific: I wrote 295 query letters about teaching positions, and I located one—just one—vacancy to suit my credentials," I said.

"One?" A fellow repeated.

"Just one?" Another said, raising an index finger.

"Yes, just one," I replied and raised my index finger.

"Holy Cow!" Another shouted.

"Did you say the job was in India, or did Paul misunderstand you?" a person said with a smile.

I chuckled and replied, "No, no, the job is this one."

"I read in the *Chronicle*," a faculty member added, "that the job market is indeed horrible these days; but precisely because it is so horrible, small schools like ours could really improve their faculty by loading up on Ph.D.s for the same salary that they would otherwise give to masters."

"That's right," I said, "I know at least fifteen Ph.D.s at Indiana who would have loved this job or another like it."

"And I bet you don't get paid that much," a bearded professor said.

"Eight thousand," I replied, "but then I have no experience in teaching, and judging from my performances in class so far, I probably have few—if any—real gifts for teaching."

"If I were you," someone advised me, "I'd tone down that modesty and let the students decide just how good or bad your teaching appears to them."

"Things here are comparatively cheap," another gentleman said, "so the low salary still goes a long way."

"They're not that cheap if you've got a troop of kids to support, to buy them boots, bikes, and baloney," another person protested.

"Maybe it's tough for a family," I said, "but not long ago I got a haircut here in Shawnee, and I only paid fifty cents for it."

"Fifty what?" Someone exclaimed.

"Fifty cents for the haircut—and three dollars for the tip," I said.

Most of the professors caressed my bald head with a glance and laughed. "I'm glad to hear that," one lady said, "because dear old Jim—that's this fellow sitting over here—can't use his canoe joke on you." She paused, then added, "Jim often compares a tight person to a canoe and claims that the difference between them is a simple one: the canoe tips."

"Even three-fifty," one fellow said, as he headed to the coffee pot to get a refill, "is cheap, for the barber not only cuts your hair but hunts for it."

While leaving the lounge that day, I remembered the words of a professor of mine at Indiana who had predicted, "You'll find the Okies to be dull and devoid of humor." He was wrong on both counts.

One morning, early in my first semester at OBU, a young lady dialed my office number and, in a charming Okie accent, said, "Since you're new here, Dr. Hanna, we'd like to introduce you to the student body. Would you be kind enough to sit for an interview for the *Bison*, that's the school newspaper?"

"I'd be delighted."

"When may I come to your office?"

"How about nine this morning?"

"That'll be fine," she said.

"I'll get a few donuts, and we'll sit and talk. It should be fun indeed."

"Sounds great; see you in a bit, Dr. Hanna. Thanks."

When she arrived, I asked her to be seated. In so doing, I prefaced her last name with the "Ms." title that was so popular in graduate school, and to it she replied, "Please don't call me that."

Even though I had often used that title in formal conversations and letters, I felt uncomfortable using it for two strange reasons: one, "Ms." was frequently associated with a disease, and two, I had typed it repeatedly in my Ph.D. dissertation as the conventional abbreviation for "manuscript." I made eye contact with her when I said, "I'm sorry, I should've asked for permission to use it."

"That's fine," she said, "now let's begin."

"Before we do, let me ask you if you'd like a cup of black coffee."

"What other colors do you have?" She asked and smiled, as her left hand scooped and flipped her short, bouncy hair away from her forehead.

"Just black."

"No, thanks," she said, poking and turning pages in a spiral notebook in search of a blank sheet.

I then offered her one of those delicate French donuts that resemble tractor tires. She thanked me again, placed a donut on a napkin, and began the interview.

Like most of the OBU students that I had met, she was neatly dressed, friendly, courteous, and prompt. She had written several uniformly intelligent questions, and in the course of my responses, she often interjected thoughtful follow-up queries. At the end of the interview, I kidded her by presenting contradictory aspects of my personality. She chimed in by kidding back, "In the labels of a fading era, would you classify yourself as a hippie or a square, Dr. Hanna?"

"Neither."

"What then are you?"

"A rhombus," I replied.

"You'd call yourself that, wouldn't you?" She said, as she stood to leave. She smiled and added, "See ya, bye."

When the issue of the *Bison* in which I was to appear hit the dorms and the Student Union, I snapped up a copy and headed to the donut shop located across the street from my office. The *Bison* had no profile of the young professor from Indiana, no picture, no headline. Not a word. The editors, I reasoned to myself, must have replaced my profile with an ad for those pointed cowboy boots or for a Chinese chicken dinner with "flied lice" at the Mandarin.

That edition of the *Bison* carried an article on the extensive faculty inbreeding at OBU and at the church-related college in general. I was surprised, even disappointed, to learn that the scholarly and progressive president of the university encouraged inbreeding. After reading the well-written article, I checked the university's catalogue and verified the writer's data. Many of those who were inbred had gone on to receive Ph.D.s from some of the country's leading universities. The school had also attracted other Ph.D.s from many well-known universities among them Iowa, Harvard, Johns Hopkins, Columbia, Michigan, Duke, Texas, Cornell, Chicago, Wisconsin. One faculty member, who had earned his doctorate at Yale and who had been a Rhodes Scholar at Oxford, left his post in political science and became Governor of Oklahoma. David Boren, a Democrat, went on to win a United States Senate seat.

Not all faculty members had such impressive credentials. Some held masters from little known regional colleges or universities, and a number of these professors had attained tenure. The minute a person with life tenure died, retired, changed professions, or moved to an administrative post, the academic dean—aware of the horrible job market for Ph.D.s—replaced the departed person with the best compatible Ph.D. that he could locate. "This replacement pattern," I was told by a faculty member who chaired OBU's active chapter of the American Association of University Professors (AAUP), "reflects the dean's concern with academic excellence. Many colleges and universities claim," he added, as we walked the grounds of the well-kept campus, "to have academic excellence, but a few more than two hundred institutions have chapters of Phi Beta Kappa. We've got several Phi Betas on our staff, and I know the dean would love to land a chapter for OBU. That seems to be one of his goals."

"Phi Beta Kappa," I said, "is a superb organization to assess a college's programs and certify their excellence or lack of it. The dean is wise to aim at such a goal."

"And it sure would be great if we achieve this goal," my colleague said, as we stopped, faced each other, and headed to separate buildings. I climbed the steps of Shawnee Hall and went to my office for a brief rest between classes.

The professors that I had come to know, whether they were Phi Beta Kappa graduates or otherwise, appeared impressive indeed. They made me feel both happy and uneasy in being involved in helping the dean build OBU into a Phi Beta Kappa caliber institution. I felt happy because I believed that to be a noble goal, but uneasy because my class performance—at least during the first three months—hindered rather than helped the dean's efforts. Some students evaluated my teaching as average; others saw it as poor; the rodeo boys often resorted to that one word reserved for the governor of Oklahoma as he inspects the aftermath of a brutal tornado: DISASTER. In remarking about my lectures, one of the rodeo boys once claimed that when I had failed to put the class to sleep, I hypnotized it. Hypnosis he defined as "the art of sleeping with the eyes open." Many of my students had recourse to this mode of sleeping. But there was also another breed of sleepers, the more conventional breed, those who shut their eyes, parted their lips with heavy tongues, and either nodded in slow motion or weaved their heads like yo-yos defying the laws of gravity.

Among this conventional breed of sleepers, there was a young man who doubled, so he told me, "as a truck driver in the off season." Usually, he would sleep most of the period, then undergo a renaissance near the end of it, at which time he would ask me to summarize in a few words what I had been struggling to say throughout the period. Usually,

I would smile and follow orders. One day, however, he napped but forgot to rise on schedule. This worried me. I felt that a round of snoring on his part might create a scene. Luckily, I didn't worry for long. The bell saved me. At the end of the period, I took the lad aside and told him of the anxiety I went through when he failed to awaken on schedule. "You know, if you had slept for one more minute, I bet you would have started snoring," I said.

"Don't worry next time, Dr. Hanna, don't worry at all," he assured me, "for I only snore when I sleep at night, but when I sleep professionally, I never snore."

This brief young man, a Texan who seemed to be made in Japan, called himself "T.D.," the truck driver. He was a likable lad whose quick and sharp "prenap" wit often delighted the students by the way it yanked and clipped whatever comical remarks I had tried to use while explaining an assignment or returning an examination or introducing a lecture on Dante, Goethe, or Thomas Mann. He read voraciously, but mainly in one category: war stories. Befriending this muscular rodeo buff was another student of mine, an exceedingly bright, sensitive, gentle, talented, and altruistic young man who also worked as a preacher. The student-preacher headed Introductions, a Christian rodeo group that specialized in "introducing" people on the rodeo circuit to Jesus Christ.

One day, the three of us rode in the student-preacher's beetle Volkswagen and drove to a rodeo in a nearby town. I sat in the front seat while T.D. sprawled in the back reading *All Quiet on the Western Front*. On the way, the student-preacher displayed his systematic knowledge of Greek and the Bible by speaking to me about people in T.D.'s spiritual condition. "The Bible in First Corinthians chapters two and three," he said, "speaks about the *psychikos*, that is the once-born natural man, the fallen person; but it also speaks about the *sarkikos*, that is the carnal man, the person who converts and becomes a Christian but who is not fully surrendered to Christ, the person who lives a life dominated by his fleshly nature. Most importantly," the student-preacher added as I listened attentively, "the Bible also speaks about the spirit-filled Christian, the *pneumatikos*, that is the person whose life is fully surrendered to God, the person whose life manifests the fruits of the Spirit. Our friend," the student-preacher said and jerked his neck as if he were head-stabbing a soccer ball, "falls into the *sarkikos* classification, and I'm really trying to help him so that he becomes a more mature, spirit-filled, spiritual Christian. I'm working on it, believe me."

"That's fine," I said, "now let's talk about you and the varied ministries in which you're involved."

Besides leading Introductions, the student-preacher ministered to a small country church that gave him, for weekends and summers, a parsonage with an outhouse and no running water. As we drove through Oklahoma's softly rolling countrysides, I kidded my student about all the "stud" images that buzz his essays like flies hovering around a mule's tail. I told him that I especially liked his extended comparison of Hamlet to an Arabian stud. He asked me about my ambitions in the world of writing, and I told him, "I'm what you might call a 'hack,' that is a writer who's trying to hack it by publishing poetry, prose, reviews, drama, and I'm trying to do all that while carrying a full teaching load here at OBU."

"To folks on the rodeo circuit," he replied, "a hack is a horse for hire, one that does all sorts of work, a worn-out stud. Now, that's not what you are?"

"Yes and no," I said.

"You mean you're not trying to write the great American novel?" He asked.

"Not yet," I said with a smile, "for now I'm struggling with the great American haiku."

As he drove on, we spoke of the country church that he ministered to, of the people who cherish, as he put it, "a warm sense of community that is one hundred years behind the times." He spoke of the various ministries that he performed: visitation, marriages, funerals, baptism, counseling—all while a junior in college and twenty years of age. He felt called to serve that country church, and that is the key requirement in the Southern Baptist denomination: the calling more so than the education, "though most of our pastors," he quickly added, "have excellent seminary training." When I expressed an amazement at the demands of his job and a strong admiration for his commitment, he informed me that many other students have similar jobs, performing identical ministries on Wednesdays and the weekends, though few drive a distance farther than the two hundred miles that he drives and few labor under such unusual living conditions.

Once at the scene of the rodeo, the student-preacher threw his money into a pool that added to forty dollars. Our truck driver friend, limping from a recent rodeo accident, stood beside me and watched. "Whatever you do," the student-preacher took me aside and said, "make sure T.D. doesn't witness to a single soul here without me being present." I didn't ask him for a reason, but he offered one anyway, "A new Christian needs to sink his roots deeper into the faith and must grow and mature before preaching to others."

"I'll do all I can," I assured the student-preacher, "to keep T.D. from witnessing to anyone."

Though my student had a bull that would have made Hemingway's whiskers stand, he rode it for eight seconds before getting dumped. He won the forty dollars. But the bull kicked his arm; it swelled slightly. When we arrived in Shawnee, we went to get it x-rayed. The cost: thirty-six dollars. Net profit: two dollars. (The other two dollars went for gas.)

"This is the perfect profit margin," the student-preacher quipped, "Wall Street does not feel threatened by it and neither do my parishioners. Threatened for different reasons, you understand." I did, or at least I felt I did. The student-preacher's eloquence, his reading knowledge of Greek (he could also read Hebrew), his wit, industry, intelligence, and tact—these traits shattered my graduate school stereotype of the country preacher.

Required chapel services were held once a week at OBU. The services featured leading Christian writers, musicians, scientists, evangelists, political theorists, theologians, legal scholars, and other minds. The chapel services, along with the strong film series and visiting artist-lecturer programs, enriched the academic programs of the university. Being a Southern Baptist institution, OBU saw itself in the tradition of the denomination's best colleges and universities among which were Baylor, Mercer, Wake Forest, Richmond, and Furman. Accordingly, the OBU chapel services frequently presented the tradition's best minds, and the academic community in Shawnee engaged those minds in a number of creative activities, activities that heightened one's interests in chapel.

Chapel speakers, for example, participated in "Chapel Talk-Back," a meeting held, not in the huge chapel, but in a smaller room in the Student Union. There, students, professors, administrators, and others who had attended the chapel presentations were invited to question, press, challenge, or congratulate the speakers on their presentations. I attended the "Talk-Back" sessions and witnessed the university's brightest students as they forced the visiting speakers to sharpen the focus of their presentations or to qualify some of their points or to reassess the implications of their arguments. I often came away from the "Talk-Back" forums proud of the articulate and cogent contributions of the OBU students and convinced that the speakers must have left the campus impressed by the intellectual force of the Shawnee school. I remember one unusually tense session when a brilliant philosophy student, clutching a yellow legal pad, stood up and played Socrates by subjecting a fellow with a Yale Ph.D. and several books to his credit to a barrage of questions that ultimately led the speaker to the uncomfortable admission that "perhaps in the interest of a meaningful concept of academic freedom, evolutionists and creationists, atheists and Christians should be invited to teach at such places as Baylor, Furman, and OBU." The student pressed the exhausted speaker by insisting, "And at Yale, too?" And to that, the speaker nodded in agreement and called on another student. The student promptly stood up and questioned the wisdom of having non-Christians teaching in Christian colleges and universities, especially those schools that strive to integrate faith with learning.

That "Talk-Back" session, along with the two cups of coffee that I had before class, worked hard on my bladder. So, before returning to my office, I virtually floated to the basement washroom in Shawnee Hall. When I came out, relieved and relaxed, I was approached by the cleaning lady who was sitting on a bench a few yards away from the washroom door.

"Hey fellow," she shouted at me, "out of herbs I grow hair. I'm an old Seminole Injeian lady, and I've got this registered with the government." She spoke rapidly as if she was receiving a dime for every word inside a minute. She continued her pace, "It's much better than you think. I guarantee you'd have a full head of hair in no time. I did it on my husband and he got hair now. Before that, the good Lord had pulled the rug from top of him; he was bald as an ice cube. It's a miracle I married him."

Shocked and speechless, I stood and stared at her. Then I told her to bring me a jar, and I promised her to try it.

"It'll cost you eight dollars," she said.

"OK, I'll pay that; I'll try anything."

"Oh, I'll guarantee you this will work. I'll bring you pictures of my husband before and after. You'll be convinced. No one can get this because I wrote Washington, and it's registered. So, for eight dollars you'd have a full head of hair in no time. It'll work, son."

"Sounds great," I offered.

"When I first noticed you bald was at a powwow in Seminole, at the armory there. I was going around the drummers dancing, following my husband. He was that one with all them feathers, leading them to the beat of the drums. And I noticed you bald. Alleluia. All those Injeians with beautiful long braided hair—and there you was, bald. There is no need for you to be bald. Now I know some hairs turn gray and others turn loose, but my, my, yours really took off. Now I've seen you here too, but your baldness really shown down there. It spoke louder, if you know what I mean. I'll bring you a pint of this stuff for eight—"

"That'll be fine with me, I'll try anything."

"Quit calling what I make anything. It's certainly something. I'm Injeian and I've got this registered with the government. It'll work. People will turn and look at you with their eyes big as the saucers of disbelief. Some people will tell you to go to Oke City and get a hairpiece, and they'll tell you that these days you can get one that you can go swimming in. What they don't tell you is what will you do if it goes off while you's swimming. Tell me, please tell me, just—"

"I'll swim after it."

"Dang it," the Indian lady fired back, "all you want to do is make fun of me."

"No, I don't; I'm a believer, after all. Aren't you?"

"I certainly am; all Injeians are; we've got the Bible now, and the White Man has the land. You ought to know that by now."

"I do, I do," I said, walking backwards, "and when you get that stuff, bring it up to my office, and I'll pay you then."

Outside the washroom, inside the classroom, peculiarities pecked on me, thanks to my abundant quirks and blunders. One day, for example, I walked into class and began a lecture on modern poetry by saying, "Modern poetry differs from the old traditional poems that I grew up writing in the schools of Milwaukee. In those days, for example, the results of a 'Senior Achievement' project at an old folks home might have been described in this manner:

> They failed in their business ventures
> They wailed and gnashed their dentures.

These words rhyme, but they're not exactly what you'd call good contemporary poetry. In the next few sessions, we'll see why, and we'll see what goes into the making of a good modern poem."

The lecture piqued the poetic sensibility of a Sac and Fox Indian, a tall, soft-spoken, and dashing gentleman whose searching and critical mind often led him to make incisive and witty comments in class discussion. Unable to attend class the following session, the Indian came by my office and slid under the door a note that said:

Dr. Hanna,
Sick wife, sick baby,
I'll be back Monday, maybe;
For a better explanation please phone
This evening at my home.

We spent four weeks discussing the elements of poetry, with particular emphasis on imagery, simile, metaphor, symbol, allegory, overstatement, understatement, irony, paradox, allusion, meaning, tone, and other concerns. At the end of the fourth week, the students asked me to share with them a poem that I had written or published and to subject it to the same critical scrutiny that we had brought to bear on the major and minor poets included in our text.

At first, I felt uneasy with their request. What if they don't like my poem? Will they destroy me in their upcoming evaluations of the course and of my performance in it? Will their evaluations—if they were negative i.e. honest— lead me back to the letter-writing, vita-tucking stage? Questions of this sort, at first, bothered me, then they tyrannized me, but they vanished when I juxtaposed them with this reasoning: My literary works have been assaulted by shrewd and rude cafe critics in Milwaukee, by bright and competitive graduate students in Bloomington, by demanding and discriminating editors at the nation's literary and academic quarterlies; so why not allow the students to read a sample and to sling their critical arrows at it?

Accordingly, I xeroxed a poem that appeared in the *Wascana Review* of the University of Regina in Canada, and I shared the poem with the students. I invited them to read it and to isolate and label in the margin the literary devices present in the poem. "Since it's your poem," one student remarked, "why don't you read it to us?"

"Before I do," I said, "let me tell you that the poem is based on what I had seen on, as its title states, 'The Streets of Tangier, Morocco.' Let's see if I can get you to participate in the experience that the poem records." The students listened as I read:

Old ladies on tour
busses wilt rapidly.

They left their "Go Big Red"
alumni caps with their wilting
wives at the Hilton, and with
golf slacks mesmerized
high over their pancake bellies,
they waddled to the *medina*
snowballing in their wake
shoe-shine boys specializing in sandals,
street peddlers boasting the
highest-low prices in town,
tour guides reeking with the sauce
and legend of the place,
newspaper boys chanting "extra, extra
read all about it" and even
pimps, surprised pimps, surprised to
be hotly in pursuit.

In the *medina*, they entered a shop,
shedding an entourage that would return
swift and sure as a
band of flies cahootsing with
a pile of dates.
They priced items in dollars,
spoke broken English, felt a
curious fluency in the dialogue.
They entered empty-headed,
emerged wearing red fezes with
black tassels
instant and proud graduates into
the Moroccan way.

They languished into a classy cafe
with transparent windows.
They smiled as their snowball,
sporting glacier proportions, melted
ever so slowly.

Inspiration comes in spurts.

That day, a local cafe-poet
began an ode:
    Little do they realize
    That we know otherwise
Hours later, they left as

the poet wrote:
A fez and a beer belly
Cohere into a classic anomaly.

I gave the students ten minutes or so to isolate the literary devices used in the poem. The sharper students had no problem labeling metaphors, overstatement, irony, paradox, and so forth; several students offered penetrating and intelligent remarks regarding the poem's tone, purpose, and humor; one student pointed to an "ill-advisedly used cliché, one that needs to be freshened or dissolved."

As the first semester neared its end, I began to assess my stay in Shawnee. I wrote this for a diary entry in early December:

> I'm certainly enjoying my stay at OBU. Many of my students are bright, courteous, hard-working, and highly motivated. Most of my colleagues seem to be learned folks, and some have significant publications. All seem to be dedicated to excellence in teaching. My teaching performance has been poor. On a scale of one to ten, with my first few days in the classroom being ten, I'd give myself a seven or an eight. And I suspect my students' evaluations will reveal that. I'll certainly have to work hard to attain level one or two, the levels of the best teachers at OBU, levels that I understand have been attained by three science professors who feed a constant stream of OBU graduates into leading medical schools and graduate programs. Poet John Ciardi was here the other day, and a number of other, nationally known, speakers are scheduled to come in the near future. Christmas will soon be here, and tomorrow I'm going to the Christmas dinner of the international students.

The person who had invited me was Nickolas, an Afro-African from Nigeria. The day of the dinner, the temperature was eleven degrees, and Nickolas came up to my apartment wearing two sweaters, a scarf, a sport coat, and an overcoat as well as one of those leather-looking hats padded with fake fur, the kind of hat that reminds one of pictures

of the Wright Brothers. After tying my necktie, I blew my
nose in a handkerchief, folded it, and placed it in my pocket.
"Dr. Hanna, why are you saving that stuff from your nose?"
Nickolas asked then added, "You should use the sink or a
paper napkin that you can throw away." I smiled as he began to complain about the English language in general. He
asked, "Dr. Hanna, could you please tell me what does it
mean when some person says, 'It's cold as a witch's teeth'?"

"I don't think you mean to say 'teeth', Nickolas, and to
tell you the truth, I really don't know." I had assumed he
was asking about the origins of the common expression.

"But you're a doctor, Dr. Hanna."

"That I am, and it means that it's very cold, and if you
think it gets cold here, Nickolas, then you ought to go up
to Wisconsin where I went to college; it's really cold up
there."

"Colder than here?"

"Much colder," I replied, "in Wisconsin they claim to get
four months that are cold and eight months that are darn
cold."

"I also heard today," Nickolas added, "a person say, 'it's
cold as hell.' Now, Dr. Hanna, I've always been taught that
hell was hot, very hot indeed."

"You're right," I said.

After he offered a few more complaints on the English
language, I added a few of my own. "In America, we often
say 'It's raining cats and dogs,' when in actuality, it never
rains these. One student from Texas told the class the other
day that in Texas, it rains 'cats, dogs, and frogs.'"

"This is unusual, very unusual, Dr. Hanna," Nickolas said
and scratched his nose that resembled a beetle Volkswagen.
He stood in the living room and stared at a huge poster of
T. S. Eliot that covered pockets of dirt and several obnox-
ious nail holes in the wall. I looked up at him as I tied my
shoes, and I glanced at his tribal marks: bars of epidermis
burnt into his coarse cheeks. Then I added another example: "Take American football. What you call football in Africa, we call soccer here. In American football, we rarely
kick the ball; in other words, we rarely use our foot. And

when we do, we call it a punt or a field goal. Still, another example," I continued, "deals with the American idea of a shot. If someone asks you if you want a shot, don't pull out a knife and stab him in self-defense, for a shot has nothing to do with a pistol or a rifle; it deals with a drink. But at a good religious college like ours, you don't need to worry about that question, even though it deals with fine spirits."

A week after that dinner, I sat in my office and conversed with a student about a course that I was scheduled to teach the next term. At one instance, I placed my feet on the desk, glanced out the opened door, and noticed the Seminole Indian lady who had sold me her recipe for growing hair. She marched in front of my office pushing a broom. "Say, Ma'am," I shouted, and the Indian lady backtracked a few steps and stepped into the office, "I've been using your hair-growing substance, and as you can see nothing is happening."

"Oh, it'll happen; it just takes time. Hair is probably growing in places you don't even notice."

"You don't mean my chest, do you? I've got lots of hair there. Any more will simply be a redundancy."

"A what?"

"A redundancy."

"A re-dunce on you," she said, raising her voice slightly, "what's the matter with you? You don't put medicine on your head to grow hair on your chest. It just takes time. A baby don't become a boy with just one bottle of milk. You need to get more of my stuff and have some of that Oral Roberts faith if you want hair."

"I see what you mean," I said.

"I mean to tell you," she added, "that my husband is the before and after example that I use. When I married him, he had as much hair as you have on the palm of your hand, and now—"

"He's got as much as I have on the back of it. Is that what you're going to say?"

"Let me see your hand," she said. I showed her my right hand; she fondled it, turned it toward the light, and said, "A bit more than that, but that alone is a big improvement. Don't you think? Ask this fellow right here."

"Oh, by the way," I said, "let me introduce you to this fellow; he's one of the university's brightest students, a premed student; his name is Mike Pontious."

"Pleased to meet you," she told Mike.

"Likewise," Mike replied.

"Where do you originate from?" She asked Mike.

"What do you mean by that?" He replied.

"Like where you from? What country did your parents come from? Like I'm a Seminole Injeian, a pure breed native American."

"Oh, I see," Mike replied and offered a little discourse on the mixture of his European ancestry.

She summed up his remarks by a question: "So, you're a mutt?"

"I never thought of it that way," Mike said, "but if you're a pure breed, I'm a mutt indeed."

"Hey that rhymes," the Indian lady said, walked out of the office, and told me, "let me know when you need more of my secret hair recipe."

"I sure will," I told her then turned to Mike and said, "that lady sold me some Indian medicine that she had formulated, and she claimed that if I applied it properly, it'll grow hair. So far it has done nothing but shine my head, waxing it, accentuating my baldness—if you know what I mean."

"Maybe," Mike said, as he began to walk out of the office, "she wants you to look brilliant, just brilliant."

At the beginning of my second year in Shawnee, I drove to a nonmilitant urologist in Oklahoma City to see about my nagging prostate. While sitting next to the fish bowl in the crowded waiting room, I wrote another "poem" for the Epitaph Factory Series. The poem (which later appeared in the *Literary Review*) read:

> He lived
> with a measure of
> touch-and-go tenderness

similar to
*Playboy* in braille
He died
waiting for the mail—

Written in behalf of the writer in American culture, the poem became my Sooner soliloquy as I waited for the mail to return from all the literary magazines in the glamorous states of California and New York to 2311 North Kickapoo in Shawnee, Oklahoma. While in Oklahoma, I wrote and mailed fiction and poetry, and I waited for replies.

My quirkiest poems seemed to get accepted rapidly. For some reason, however, they rarely appeared. One San Francisco editor (to whom I had sent a cover letter that read: "Here are some poems, you figure them out, all I do is write the stuff,") scribbled an acceptance note and promised to forward me copies of the issue of *Grunt* in which my stuff was to appear. That acceptance note came twenty months before I had journeyed to Oklahoma. Given my experiences with "Little" and literary magazines, I reasoned that *Grunt* had either died or the editor responds to his mail only on leap years. Three other manuscripts of mine—poetry, fiction, essay—were out, and they had been out for a long time and I had not heard a word on them: no mail, no rejections, no acceptances, no reprints to show to friends. Simply silence. And about that silence I finally decided to do something and to do it with my students.

One cold Friday evening, I telephoned seven of my brightest and most creative students at OBU (a university that had a high number of exceedingly capable students) and invited them over to my apartment for coke, pizza, and a couple of hours to talk about the state of the arts in Shawnee. Little did I realize that the couple of hours, starting at ten in the evening, would breaststroke through the night and surface at seven o'clock in the morning when the students and I found ourselves in a truck stop eating pancakes, drinking coffee, and, strangely enough, waiting for a grocery store to open.

When the students arrived at my apartment, I proposed the idea of giving birth to a literary magazine. Immediately we began to look for a name. We dismissed the serious and ponderous titles of this or that "review" or "quarterly" or "journal" and opted for the more creative titles of the "artsy-craftsy" variety, as one person put it. We recited the Lord's Prayer and the "Star Spangled Banner" and noted that both of these grand works were heavily milked for titles. Then we thought of continuing *Cantaloupe*, the magazine that I had helped edit in graduate school back at Indiana University, the magazine that was a fresh and juicy literary organ, the monthly that turned out to be irregular. But the memory of the weird San Francisco suicide of a *Cantaloupe* editor led me to veto the proposition of resurrecting that organ.

The fruit cantaloupe, however, gave us ideas. We tried *Pomegranate* for a title, and the image of pearls appeared attractive and suggestive. This title endured for a good while. In the end, we rejected it, for the structured pearls of the pomegranate reminded one of the participants, a potential editor, of the teeth of her former boyfriend.

When the coke bottle was being passed around the room for the third time, I ended up with it. It was nearly empty—actually, it had the collective spit of the entire crew. So, I took it to the kitchen and brought another. On the way back, I picked up Charles Darwin's *Voyage of the Beagle*, which I had been reading all week; I had left it open to the 17 November 1835 entry that records Darwin's times in the Tahitian islands. I took the book and the coke bottle and then read the following passage: "Before we laid ourselves down to sleep," Darwin wrote in his diary for that rainy November day, "the elder Tahitian fell on his knees, and with closed eyes repeated a long prayer in his native tongue. He prayed as a Christian should do, with fitting reverence, and without fear of ridicule or any ostentation of piety. At our meals," Darwin continued, "neither of the men would taste food, without saying beforehand a short grace. Those travellers who think that a Tahitian prays only when the eyes of the missionary are fixed on him, should have slept with us that night on the mountain-side. Before morning it rained very heavily; but the good thatch of banana-leaves kept us dry."

Immediately after I had finished reading that passage, someone beat me to the punch, "There's our title: *Bananas.*"

"Well," I said, "I was going to suggest 'thatches,' but bananas as a title has potential."

"Doc, go ahead and suggest 'thatches' and it would be our pleasure to ignore your suggestion." All the students laughed at that remark.

"We can subtitle *Bananas* by somehow using the word 'thatches,'" someone added, "and in so doing, we'd please both of you and Darwin too. Will this idea dance in Shawnee?"

"How about *Bananas: A Thatch of Creativity* for a title?" A young lady said.

"Great," a second stated.

"That title will definitely dance in Shawnee," a third added.

"You mean, it will definitely powwow in Shawnee," a fourth said.

"Huh," a fifth snorted.

For a good while, we worked over the metaphor; we massaged it, felt its pulse and potential. We accepted it and decided to print, as a sliver of a thought on the inside cover of each issue, this little passage: "Before morning it rained very heavily; but the good thatch of banana-leaves kept us dry." In so doing, we reasoned, the readers would be invited every issue to see the origins and drift of our metaphor, indeed purpose.

Since my apartment was located on Shawnee's grand old Kickapoo, we decided to call our press the Kickapoo Spur Press and to use a boot with a spur on it for a logo. This decision came easy, but for the next seven hours, until daybreak in fact, we toiled on the wording of the preamble to be used in the first issue of *Bananas*. Here is the result of our labors: "Footnote to the artistic sensibility of the age: This might serve as a good statement of what *Bananas: A*

*Thatch of Creativity* is all about. Heir to that fine and imposing tradition of the 'Little' magazine, *Bananas* will—at its best—prod the age's sensibility. It will stride along, tall and handsome and proud. At its worst, the stout boot will pinch, and *Bananas* would limp along, slow and weak. We pledge to do our best now that we've come of age."

At seven in the morning we headed to a truck stop for coffee and pancakes and a period of waiting. At about nine, we invaded a grocery store. Mission, not impossible but incredible. We wanted to buy one hundred or more bananas. We entered the store, hesitated momentarily, then grabbed a wagon and pushed it to the banana pile. We took all the bananas in the store: a total of ninety-seven bananas. "We have a monkey farm over here in Tecumseh," we told the clerk and all the curious people who had filed in front of us, behind us, and to our sides. We then took the bananas and drove to the Building and Grounds Department of the university. Once there, we asked for, and received, a stepladder. We carried the bananas and the ladder, and we walked to a patch of sunny grass located near the cafeteria. There, our staff photographer whom we had called and appointed from a phone at the truck stop met us. We dumped the bananas, positioned them carefully so that they spelled out the word *Bananas*. Having done that—but not before we had, in the words of T. S. Eliot ". . . a hundred indecisions . . . a hundred visions and revisions,"—the photographer climbed the ladder and photographed the word.

Numerous students who were leaving the cafeteria gathered to observe the photographer at work. We distributed most of the bananas to the curious students and instructed them to peel and eat them. As they did, the photographer clicked several shots of them eating the bananas. We felt that if we published the pictures of the students eating the bananas, we would sell at least seventy or eighty copies in Shawnee alone. We reasoned that most, if not all, people would buy the forum in which their picture appeared no matter what the forum was about. The photographer requested the biggest uneaten banana in the bunch. As the students began to leave, the photographer told us of his plans,

"I'm going to lay this banana flat and photograph it in the lab; then I'll take the negative spelling out the word '*Bananas*' and superimpose it on this large banana. It'll be cool." "Your bananas will be cool if you put them in the refrigerator," a student said as he chewed his final bite and headed in the direction of the stately library.

Happy and haggard, stuffed with pancakes and bananas, the editorial board directed me to send out news releases to the *Writer* in Boston, *Writer's Digest* in Cincinnati, the *Small Press Review* in California, and *Margins* in Milwaukee. I agreed. And given the phallic images associated with bananas, I offered to work into the news release a passage addressed to the graduate students urging them to restrain their stream of consciousness, avoiding, if at all possible, the marshes of erotica. I also pledged to plead with the old ladies who delight in doggerels to spare us from their literary output.

While waiting to be listed in national forums, we collected literary and artistic works from the editorial staff and from friends of the staff living in central Oklahoma. We also solicited financial donations and used books from members of the university community. We sold the books at a campuswide book sale that we felt might help the students at OBU develop a book consciousness. With two hundred and fifty three dollars in our bank account, we decided to go to press. What we had was not much, but then we were a "Little" magazine.

We bought the cover and the paper for the magazine, typeset the prose and poetry, solicited graphics for the cover and other parts, designed and pasted all the items so that *Bananas* was camera ready. For three hundred copies, we paid two hundred and forty eight dollars. That price included trimming and stapling. When we went to the printer to deliver the magazine, we received a five dollar parking ticket that pushed our bank account back to zero.

When the magazine appeared, I wrote an article entitled "*Bananas* and the Kickapoo Spur Press" that appeared in the *Small Press Review* of Paradise, California. Many literary submissions came in as a result of that article. We rejected most of them with this note that led to dollar notes: "Sorry, try us again. *Bananas* one dollar."

One day the staff took a signed copy of *Bananas* to present to the owner of Kickapoo Sam's Coney Island, a small restaurant where many of our editorial meetings were held. It was a sad day for the Kickapoo, for some of the creditors were there hauling away tables and chairs and grills. He stood and watched them. The holes in his socks were large as eggs. There was anguish in his bloodshot eyes that stared three yards ahead, but must have seen those distances that come with the reality of an overwhelming defeat. "Would our magazine," I asked myself as we were leaving, "be like the Kickapoo's venture: Here today and gone tomorrow?"

From the three hundred copies that we had published, we sold eighty-eight copies in two days, and in less than a year, we sold all the available copies and received subscriptions for more issues from many places among them the New York Public Library and the University of Wisconsin in Madison. I mentioned these places when I tried to convince the head librarian at OBU to buy a copy of *Bananas* for the library. The librarian refused to use a mere dollar of library money for a copy, even though many OBU faculty members and students were published in it. By contrast, the academic dean wrote me a note praising the work of *Bananas*.

"Should some folks come along ten years from now to do research on Shawnee culture in the seventies," an editorial board member said during a staff meeting, "they'll have to go to the interlibrary-loan system to get a copy of *Bananas* from Wisconsin or New York or Washington; OBU, where the magazine was born and edited, would not have a copy, thanks to the enthusiasm of our librarian." The librarian's response to *Bananas* disappointed the staff.

What delighted the staff, however, was the seriocomic reaction of an administrator; he called me into his office and warned me to be cautious; he was referring, not to a poem or a photograph, not to an essay, not even to a short story or a graphic, but to the notes on the contributors which we entitled "They Came Our Way." For one of OBU's brightest and most accomplished scholars we wrote: "D. C.

Peck holds a Ph.D. in Literature from Ohio University. He has recently completed research for a forthcoming book in Elizabethan history. He considers himself to be a leading authority on Queen Elizabeth's period." The administrator smiled and assured me that he "enjoyed *Bananas*." He offered to give us financial support for future issues. "The magazine is good for OBU," he added.

*Bananas* brought the university a small measure of positive publicity. One day a reporter from the town's only daily the *Shawnee-News Star* came to my office to interview me. She stayed for an hour or so, asked me all sorts of questions for an extensive feature that she had planned to do on the magazine. After the interview, she asked to use my office phone in order to call a photographer. Then she asked me to call a young lady who might be willing to get in the picture and pretend that she was buying *Bananas* from me. Well, I called one of my favorite students, but she was out of the dorm; then I tried another and another. No luck. I tried one more and slammed the phone in anger, bit my lower lip, and said with the whistling whisper of the "s" sound, "Nuts, nuts, nuts." The reporter, a personable lady in her sixties perhaps, a veteran of thirty-three years of journalism experience at the Shawnee paper, looked up at me and said, meekly and clearly and tenderly, "Dr. Hanna, Dr. Hanna, I would like you to call a student—not a squirrel."

"I'll be happy to," I said, "I'm sorry, I really am."

At last I thought. I stepped out of my office and stood in the hall for a minute or so. I cornered a beautiful red-haired cheerleader from Wichita, Kansas, and she agreed to pose buying *Bananas*. It took a minute or less to entice her. That week's Sunday paper published the picture and a long feature on the magazine under the headline:

FIRST EDITION PEELED AND REVEALED?
OBU "*BANANAS*" LITERARY MAGAZINE UNVEILED

After unveiling the first issue, we set out to achieve our next goal of publishing two more issues in order to qualify for a grant from the Coordinating Council of Literary Magazines. We worked hard, and before the end of the academic year we completed the third issue. In time, *Margins*, the forum that in the seventies had authoritatively chronicled and evaluated America's "Little" magazines and small-press books, published an article on our magazine and the Kickapoo Spur Press. Several OBU professors and two students were praised in the *Margins* piece. William R. Mitchell's poetry—mature, incisive, concise, quietly powerful, and finely crafted—highlighted each of the issues; as editors, we were pleased to publish in our fledgling magazine the work of an absolutely first-rate poet.

One day, several editors from *Bananas* and a number of their friends initiated me into their Sacred Order of the Bison, an exclusive club composed of the men who cared for the Bison, the school's mascot, and who represent the closest thing to an official fraternity at OBU. "Chips" was their Greco-Okie name; parody—in the honorable tradition of Harvard's Hasty Pudding—was their main, and often cleverly executed, concern. Initiation day, I had read in the *Shawnee-News Star* an Associated Press article dealing with the Beaver Chamber of Commerce that was reported to be sending a cow chip delegation to Oklahoma City. The delegation planned to climb the steps of the capitol and advertise their annual chip throwing contest. The folks from Beaver, the article noted, "are coming complete with a wagon load of authentic, aromatic cow chips." That day, little did I know that I too would be involved in cow chip festivities as part of a traditional—but extra special—convocation parody.

The ceremony was simple enough. After most of the students gathered in the university's largest auditorium, the men of Chips marched from the rear of the auditorium and headed to the stage as the organist played—off key, of course—"Pomp and Circumstance." All the men—whether they were tall, dark, and handsome; short, fat, and fair; or another combination of these traits—wore dark suits, tight vests, and flashy hats. One young man marched in hoisting the dreaded text used in the university's required unit in Western Civilization, a twelve-credit unified history-literature course that had a reputation for being grueling, systematic, and excellent. Another young man clutched a tray. The rest of the men carried picks or shovels or brooms. All had declared a nasty war on laughter; all reflected the spontaneity of anger that is often generated by a parking ticket. All strode in, stern and statuesque, with a wink at the mischievous.

Once on stage, the master of ceremonies, presumably the greatest chip of them all, straddled a podium and blasted out the name of a new chip, congratulated him, and then paraded his credentials. While this was happening, an old chip left the stage, marched to the place where the new recruit was sitting, escorted him back to the stage, and finally placed a hat on his head. The hat symbolized the new chip's coming of age. After all the student members were tapped, the jovial, witty, dignified, and highly regarded president of OBU and the strict but kiddable vice-president for student affairs—cx-officio members of Chips—were told to step up to the stage. They followed orders. Dr. Jeff Black, a gifted professor of biology, a popular teacher and a well-published scholar, was tapped next.

"Finally, we have," I remember hearing the master of ceremonies say, "a young scholar who as a boy walked the mean streets of Milwaukee, land of milk and beer, a young professor who received a B.S. before a Ph.D., a young man who believes that reading *Bananas* will curtail your chances of getting an appendix transplant, a young man who refuses to go to Shawnee's best movie house because they've had the same thing running all the time (air-conditioning), this doctor of philosophy and professor of English literature is none other than the literary flagship the SS Hanna."

The old chip assigned to come down and escort me to the stage was the one carrying the tray. Rather than bring it down to my seat area, he gracefully handed it over to the president of the university who was now solemnly standing on the stage front and center. To everyone's delight, the president clutched it and waited for me to walk the aisle and climb the stairs. When I finally arrived on stage, a bearded young man positioned, with his elbows fluttering dramatically, a cowboy hat on my head.

"What you're about to see," the master of ceremonies said, "you often see in crowded elevators and in the pro football draft." After a long pause, he said, "The SS Hanna, the last chip will be the first one out. Watch him navigate us out of here." As I began to march, the master of ceremonies said, alluding to an old test score, "Hanna, I still remember that fifty-two, I do, I do."

Later that afternoon while checking my mail, I ran into the OBU president who informed me that being inducted into Chips "speaks highly of the manner you've endeared yourself to the students. This parody tradition has been going on at OBU for years." He shook my hand and said, "It'll be interesting to see how the *Bison* reports the ceremony in this week's paper."

"It sure would," I said, respectfully thanked the departing president, and began to open my mail. That afternoon, the mail consisted of a copy of Anne Sexton's *An Awful Rowing Towards God*—a book that had earned the label "urgent" on my summer reading list, a list that was loaded with spiritual items—, two self-addressed rejection letters (SARL) and a "Marked Copy" of *Writer's Digest* that published an excerpt from the news release announcing the birth and the literary needs of *Bananas*. The excerpt unleashed America's prolific nonwriters, the unsung heroes of postal subsidy.

Several weeks after the Chips ceremony, I went to OBU's graduation exercises. For those exercises, all faculty members dressed in the "academic regalia," as one scholar kept calling our colorful uniforms. A distinguished professor who seemed to love ceremony read us our marching orders, and when the exact moment arrived, we marched to the auditorium and we marched down its aisles: slow and solemn and self-conscious. We sat in the front sections and listened to an address by an academician, then a charge to the graduates given by another academician, and then the roll call of four hundred graduates. The auditorium's thousand plus seats were packed. Following the speeches and the roll call, there was the "hooding of the university's honor graduates," a long and involved ceremony. Having served on the university's Honors Committee and having interviewed, examined, and read the honor graduates' often outstanding theses—required and exhausting works that were always refereed by recognized scholars at major universities—I felt pleased to be a part of that ceremony. Honor students of OBU were truly a gifted lot who could excel at Harvard, Yale, Princeton, or Oxford. They were that good.

Throughout my stay in Shawnee, I attended the University Baptist Church where a learned evangelical pastor often preached biblical sermons that reminded me of what chapel services might have been like in the early years of Harvard and Yale. During my last Sunday service in Shawnee, I found myself reflecting on what might be labeled as "the strangest archives" for the historian of colonial America. True, I reasoned to myself, the diaries written during the colonial period are essential for the historian; true, the letters and minutes of important personalities and events are essential; true, the newspaper accounts and the literary documents of the period are essential; true, the biographies of leading figures and institutions are essential; but there is something about the cold print or script of the diaries, letters, minutes, news items, poems, sermons, and biographies that fails to capture a feel for the intensely religious atmosphere of the period. My reasoning—or, should I say, my wandering imagination—snapped to this conclusion: the least tapped, but perhaps the most promising, archives for the historian of colonial America may be found, not in conventional sources, but in unconventional ones, the most popular of which is the evangelical church of today where the colonial religious experience, with its biblical anchor and with its varied manifestations and revivals, is constantly being relived. Yet—and in this realization I saw the making of a modest "note" for a scholarly journal such as the *William and Mary Quarterly*—the bright and skeptical scholars of today spend little, if any, time in these extraordinary archives.

I spent the summer months in Amherst, Massachusetts, writing poetry on a postdoctoral grant from the National

Endowment for the Humanities. On Sundays, I attended either the quaint Baptist church in Amherst or the historic Congregational church in nearby Northampton, the church that was led for twenty-three years by Jonathan Edwards, my favorite Puritan thinker. At Amherst, beautiful Amherst, I worked on "The Muttering Retreats," a long poem in which I chart, among other concerns, the contours of agony in a brutal age, an agony that permits a television correspondent to exchange, readily and articulately, the horrible categories of suffering for words and pictures. For days I chiseled away at such metaphors that compare agony to a coal that could burn a hand or blacken it, but that could also bring warmth to a shivering human soul. By summer's end the poem remained in an unfinished state, a literary fetus, as it were. When I left Amherst, I had just completed the poem's fourth section entitled "An Acoustical Mirage." It begins:

> Blessed are those who
> Love babies and hate tumors:
> Tiny growing tumors choke life,
> Colossal ones salute it.

Before I exchanged Shawnee for Amherst, the dean—in keeping with the guidelines of the American Association of University Professors—had sent me a letter informing me that OBU might not be in a position to renew my contract because of declining enrollment and realignment of tenured personnel. The university had many excellent facets, and I hated the thought of leaving it. At the same time, I knew that I did not deserve to stay at OBU, for my overall performance had failed to measure up to that of most professors. Responding to my resignation note, the top three administrators overlooked my shortcomings and sent me detailed letters that commended my work and cited aspects of it that had impressed them. The administrators' generosity, professionalism, and sensitivity pleased me. At Amherst, I often read their letters. One day, I called my mother in Milwaukee, explained to her the concept of tenure, and told her that OBU was not in a position to keep me long enough to consider me for tenure. "That's good," she snapped, "maybe that'll force you to change professions, and if you do that, see if you can do it without going back to school." She, once again, trotted out my brothers-in-law as examples of those whose education advanced their status in life, enabling them to move from the inner city to the suburbs, to buy houses with big lawns, swimming pools, fireplaces, and garages.

In searching for another job, I followed the conventional approach. I sent out another fleet of vitas and inquiry letters. The search led to a peculiar job at a little college on the prairies of Sterling, Kansas. In Oklahoma, the diligent student assistant who had typed my letters always told me to "expect a miracle"; once, she abbreviated my rank in a manner that would have pleased my mother, for in so doing, the assistant left out the periods. She, in effect, transformed my identity from an Assistant Professor to a proctologist. That transformation was on paper.

At some point during the journey from Shawnee to Amherst to Sterling, I met and fell in love with a registered nurse with green eyes and olive-colored skin. We married, and we began a "new" life in central Kansas. In Amherst, the land bulges bosomlike; in Kansas, it has muscle tone. It took a while for me to adjust to the lay of the land and the joys and tensions of married life. My new job, however, required me to make an instant adjustment, one that transformed my identity in a serious way.

CHAPTER THREE
# Kansas:
# Coaching Football and
# Marketing Poetry

In order to clinch that teaching position in Kansas at a time when jobs for Ph.D.s were still scarce, I had agreed not only to teach English but also to serve as an assistant football coach for the Warriors of Sterling College. As an undergraduate football player, I enjoyed the sport and earned a varsity letter in it. My pursuit of the doctorate, however, had alienated me from what I often called "the locker room culture." In Kansas, I found myself in the midst of that culture once again—but this time the culture had an "upper room" motif, one that integrated coaching with Christianity.

From near the tower of Cooper Memorial, a huge stone structure built in 1887 by a hardy bunch of Scottish Presbyterians, I frequently gazed at Sterling, a rural town of two thousand people living in a square mile area. Its downtown consists of a row of shops and offices among them a clothing shop, two small banks, a savings and loan, two drug stores, a weekly newspaper, a bakery, three restaurants, two physicians and a physician's assistant, a barbershop, two grocery stores, and four lawyers. Most houses in town are well-kept clapboard structures of varying sizes. Doctors, lawyers, bankers, retired farmers, business leaders, professors live in attractive houses that are located near inexpensive houses or trailers, and this is so because the town has no zoning laws. Sterling's residents and their elected officials are not disturbed by such an arrangement, for they see themselves as modest people meshed into a town with an uncomplicated and decent life-style. Every year, the vast fields around Sterling dress in their "amber waves of grain" and sway to the tune of "O Beautiful for Spacious Skies," and almost every evening, the sun, resembling a Christmas tree ornament, hangs and dips below the horizon.

The college community of five hundred students and forty faculty members defines the cultural tone of the town, and it defines it in Christian terms. And the town easily follows the lead. Besides the large United Presbyterian Church, there is a Methodist, an Assembly of God, an African Methodist Episcopal (AME) Church, a Reformed Presbyterian Church, and two Baptist churches in town.

In large cities, such concerns as softball teams or bowling leagues are usually staffed by the working classes who frequent the local bars. Not in Sterling, Kansas. Physicians, lawyers, and bankers, for example, form a major part of the town's softball team; these players are cheered by their wives—and only their wives—for the people in town have no interest in adult summer softball. Like most other small towns in Kansas, Sterling worships on Friday nights in autumn at the shrine of high school football, and on Saturday it returns to the same stadium to witness the Warriors of Sterling College at work.

When I visited the campus for an interview, the head football coach was on a recruiting trip; so the president of the college, a former football player who was drafted by the Los Angeles Rams, explained to me my coaching duties. Early in July the head coach wrote me and confirmed the president's explanations. "I am going to ask you," the coach said in part, "to work with the kicking game, defensive ends, and assist . . . with the defense." Then he went on to in-

form me about the program: "We are members of the KCAC
[Kansas College Athletic Conference] and affiliated with the
NAIA [National Association of Intercollegiate Athletics]. We
feel we have great facilities for a small college and a good
academic program. We have much to contribute to our student athletes, but most of all the challenge"—and it is this
challenge that heightened my interest in the coaching job—
"of making men out of boys and introducing them to the
idea of total commitment which, in my opinion, starts with
a spiritual commitment to Christ." I had committed my
life to Christ as a boy growing up in a conservative church
in Milwaukee. I drifted away from that commitment, but
in time, I rowed back and discovered new dimensions and
depth in a life challenged by the demands of the cross.
Coaching football promised to add yet another dimension.

   As I reflected on the coach's letter, I knew that working
on his staff would be an experience different from what I
had witnessed as a football player at a large secular university (where our coach asked us before each game to bow
our heads for a moment of silence, but he refused to lead
us in prayer lest he offend the non-Christians on the team)
and different from what I had observed on my occasional
strolls to the athletic fields at Amherst where the New England Patriots practiced during the latter days of summer.

   "Welcome to Sterling, America," the head coach said as
he gripped my hand and pumped my arm while standing in
front of the field house. He led me to his brightly lit air-
conditioned office. On his desk was a small movie projec-
tor, and a few feet away hung a calendar-size movie screen          ·
and a blackboard. They were flanked by an assortment of
framed pictures of former athletes that he had coached.
Newspaper clippings, letters, and diplomas, all framed in
inexpensive dark tin frames and rimmed by a yellow band,
cluttered the other walls. Football, basketball, and golf trophies sat on the bookshelves that hugged the walls around
his desk. Several wooden plaques with gilded insignia hung
above the metal file cabinet in a corner of the office. Two
feet above the movie screen a framed picture of Christ dangled and tilted forward so that he looked not at the wall

opposite him, but at the people sitting below. Taped to the bottom of the frame and lettered in blue caps were these words: THE MASTER COACH.

While visiting with the head coach, I learned that Jesus Christ was indeed the Master and Savior of his life and that his mission as a coach led him to share Christ with his players at every turn. His program was committed, above all, to the glory and honor of God, and he expected his coaches to endorse that commitment and to introduce it to the athletes many of whom were non-Christians or backsliding Christians. As the coach shared with me his Christian testimony and concern, my eyes caught the headline of a framed yellowish newspaper clipping that boasted of his professional football draft by the Washington Redskins. Impressed, and in a curious way proud, I continued listening and I assured the coach that I endorsed his philosophy and looked forward to helping him implement it during the forthcoming season.

As a first step in implementing his total commitment program, the head coach asked me to pursue with the people of the Baptist church in Raymond, Kansas, a nearby farming community of less than two hundred people, the possibility of having an all-day preseason retreat on the grounds of the church. The players were to report on a Saturday in late August and the retreat would be the next day beginning with the worship service. The people of Raymond were delighted by the opportunity to serve the football team, and they agreed to prepare food and refreshments for about eighty players. They also asked me to deliver the Sunday morning message. I thanked them and agreed to their request.

Retreat day I gave a long address in that little country church crowded by more than one hundred individuals, among them all-conference players, campus heroes, nervous high school stars, returning veterans, four coaches, and active or retired farmers and their wives. My message was directed primarily at the players. I urged them to build their intellectual, spiritual, moral, and physical houses on solid rock, and not on sand where the whims of fame and delu-

sion would wash them away. Late in the message, I must
have thought that I was speaking to a collection of Rhodes
scholars from Amherst, Harvard, and Yale, for I lapsed into
quotations from Plato's *Republic,* Milton's *Paradise Lost,*
and Eliot's "The Love Song of J. Alfred Prufrock." The long
passages from Plato and Milton appeared to have transformed the church into a studio for a Sominex commercial.
The Prufrock passage, however, woke them up. I weaved
the passage into my concluding remarks, remarks that I had
tried to use in focusing the spiritual momentum of the retreat with the goals of the impending football season. "Now,
gentlemen," I said to the assembled athletes, "will you, 'after tea and cakes and ices,/Have the strength to force the
moment to its crisis?' " The moment being: the readiness
for total commitment that the football program demanded,
a commitment that, in the words of the head coach, "starts
with a spiritual commitment to Christ."

After the service, the players devoured the fried chicken,
ate cake, and drank iced tea on the lawn of the church; the
coach then divided the squad into several units for informal
games of softball and volleyball. When the players returned
to the church's auditorium, they split into two groups: of-
fense and defense. The groups outlined goals for themselves
for the season ahead. Following that session, the head coach
gathered both groups and introduced an assistant coach who,
in turn, addressed the squad on the problem of pride and
the athlete, drawing careful distinctions between the haughty
pride that "goeth before destruction" and the benign pride
that comes from a job well-done. "And whatever ye do in
word or deed," the assistant coach concluded, using St. Paul's
advice to the Colossians as recorded in the King James version of the Scriptures, "do all in the name of the Lord Jesus,
giving thanks to God and the Father by him."

That advice certainly governed my life and the life of the
head coach who rose and echoed the thoughts of his assistant. He amplified them by saying that some of the young
men on the squad might not know Christ as the Lord and
Savior of their lives, some probably never had the opportunity to commit their lives to him, others might have in-

vited him into their hearts but neglected to follow his com-
mandments. "You might," the head coach said, "leave the
program early in the season, or you might stay with us until
the last game in the cold days of November. Whatever the
case," he assured his players, "it will be impossible for any
of you to remain with us long and not to know what we—
the coaches and the Christian players—believe to be the
'Way, the Truth and the Life,' and why we hold to that belief." The coach warned that on football fundamentals and
skills, the squad will work in a most prayerful manner,
knowing full well that the talents of the players were gifts
entrusted to them by their Father in heaven. "We'll work,"
he said resorting to a spiritual saying, "like it all depends
on us, and pray like it all depends on God."

At six o'clock Monday morning, even as darkness lingered in the lonesome prairies, the players began to display
their gifts in the first of the hated two-a-day workouts,
grueling workouts consisting of running, push-ups, sit-ups,
exercises for the neck, the thighs, the shoulders, the legs,
the arms. I strolled in and out of the lines with my hands
tucked in the pockets of my Sterling Warriors' wind-
breaker; as I paced, I heard the men heaving breaths of ex-
haustion. When the team broke up into special groups, I
drilled my unit according to the instructions that were given
to me on an index card by the head coach. Following the
group workouts, there were team drills and more exercises,
more running—running in place, running forward, running
backward, running to the left and running to the right—
more wind sprints, push-ups, sit-ups, deep knee bends, and
crab walks that degenerated, to paraphrase Eliot's Prufrock,
into scuttling across the floors of silent grass.

Later that afternoon, the players repeated the exercise and
special drill cycles, and they groaned while doing it. "Two-
a-day workouts are a pain, a pain, a pain in the—," an athlete moaned as he struggled down to touch his left ankle.
I ignored his allusion to Gertrude Stein and shouted at him,
"Delete the expletive." As I sauntered towards the front line,
I heard him say, "Sorry, coach." At first, I felt slightly awkward issuing that command, but with each practice, my

awkwardness melted, my confidence grew, my grip on my authority as a coach firmed up, my knowledge of the players increased. In time, I even began to "enjoy" the cries of the coyotes of central Kansas. Throughout the morning and afternoon sessions, the players worked hard; their common goal was to avoid "sitting on the bench," for after all, they were football players, not ambitious lawyers.

In the evenings following each of the ten two-a-day sessions, the players and coaches met in two classrooms for "chalk talk" and films. During those sessions, the coaches reviewed the play book, diagraming plays and defenses, using x's and o's and arrows. They gave special emphasis to the offensive plays or defensive strategy to be introduced in the next day's practice. At the completion of the first of the two-hour workouts, the coaching staff drove to the town's only donut shop for coffee and evaluation of the morning practice.

At those coffee sessions I came to learn that the entire coaching staff supported the head coach's total commitment program. At one of these sessions, the head coach informed us that he had asked a local pastor, a tall, strong former athlete at Geneva College in Pennsylvania who worked at Sterling's Reformed Presbyterian church, to serve as the team chaplain. His primary responsibility was to address the squad on a spiritual matter every Thursday following the workout.

Before the team's opening game against the Bulldogs of McPherson College, the chaplain gave a Thursday message in which he urged the players to develop their physical and spiritual lives in the light of God's Word. He urged those who did not know Christ as personal Lord and Savior to come to him, confess their sins, and dedicate the season, indeed their lives, to his glory. His message, in effect, stated: it is one thing to play for your own glory; it is another to play for the glory of your school and coaches; still it is another to play for the glory of the one who gave you all the skills and strength at your command. It is a joy to struggle and endure for the glory of the Master Coach.

That message continued the spiritual tone set at the Raymond retreat. When the team absorbed its first defeat on a windy Saturday night in September, few players sensed glory in life under the Master Coach. McPherson College's 10–0 upset stunned and humiliated our athletes, their spirits appeared to be low; they entered the dressing room with their heads hanging; their helmets slapping their thighs; their cleats rhythmically crunching the cement walk leading to the dressing room, playing, as it were, a requium for defeat. When the players assembled in a dressing room that was silent as a coffin, the head coach asked a student manager to close the door; then he stood on a bench and gazed at a platoon of players hunched forward with their helmets crouching between their feet. "Men, let's bow our heads," he said, and in a slow, strident voice, he offered a warm and sensitive prayer, thanking God for preserving both teams from injury and asking him to teach the Warriors the appropriate lessons to be gained from defeat. Through the prayer, he assured the players that God loves them; that though they may feel dejected and disappointed, they should not feel lonely or depressed.

All that was Saturday evening. Sunday was the Lord's day: no films, no drills, no meetings. Monday at two o'clock, the coaching staff—minus the team chaplain—gathered in the office of the head coach and studied films of the previous game and the next opponent. At three o'clock, the head coach closed the door of the office, picked the phone off the hook, and began a time of Scripture reading, sharing, and prayer. We prayed for individual players, the team, the college, the coaches, the community, and the nation. The head coach usually selected the Scripture lesson and led us in the devotions.

Most players, our head coach believed, hesitate to confide their problems in college counselors, pastors, parents, but they happily seek the football coaches. During the course of our weekly Monday fellowships, for example, the head coach asked us to pray for an excellent player who told him of his drinking problem; he also urged us to pray for other players who confessed to him their hesitation to walk with the Lord; he even asked us to pray for a star player who

was having "girl friend problems." Ten years after gradu-
ating from college, most players—the head coach felt and
I certainly agreed—might vaguely recall their English
teachers or their education instructors or their psychology
professors, but they will vividly remember their coaches.
The contact and trust, therefore, that coaches established
with their players were certainly critical, and at almost every
turn, our head coach demonstrated to the coaching staff and
to the players that the presence of Christ will foster, and
not frustrate, the ideal player-coach relationship.

After losing the opening game, the team won the next
four games; they looked particularly impressive in disman-
tling the Swedes of Bethany College who came to Sterling
with three wins and no defeats. The most critical victory,
however, resulted from a shoot out in Dodge City against
St. Mary of the Plains, the defending conference champs
whose quick and powerful running backs might have excelled at Notre Dame. With four victories and one defeat,
we crossed the season's halfway point in second place, second only to the Falcons of Friends University, the boys from
the big city—Wichita.

Preparing the team for the trip to Wichita was a tiring
but pleasant task. We studied and showed them several films
of Friends University, we worked them hard in practice, and
our chaplain related his Thursday message to the Christian's confrontation with difficult problems. In the dressing
room prior to the game, the head coach gave a brilliant ora-
tion warning the players that during the ensuing battle, they
will experience almost every emotion there is in life: joy,
sorrow, pain, frustration, hope, dejection, satisfaction, long-
ing, loneliness, glee. "Whatever the case," the coach said,
"you must keep your cool, you must fight hard, block hard,
run hard, tackle, hit, hit, hit!" Following the emotional peak
of the speech, the coach asked one of the assistant coaches
to offer a word of prayer. We waited in the dressing room
for the marching band to leave the field. That afternoon,
the pregame line to the urinals was uncommonly long.

It was a tough first half with the Falcons holding a slight
lead. At halftime after going over strategy and adjustments,

the head coach let rip a Vince Lombardi-style tirade—minus the expletives. The peppery speech led me to conclude that our coach, like most other coaches, believed that a loud voice made a sound argument. For a while, the half-time speech convinced the players, for they went out and promptly scored a quick touchdown and took the lead. In the end, two (properly called) offside penalties inside the Falcons' thirty yard line proved costly in our team's final drive for the winning touchdown.

In the dressing room immediately after the game, the coach had a word with the players and then led the team in prayer. It was his classic prayer, thanking God for the safety of both squads, assuring the players that God loves them, and imploring the Lord to clarify the lessons of defeat. In the coaches' dressing room that day, we dressed in spooky silence. When Friends' head coach came to congratulate us on the dazzling performance of our quarterback Mike Danski who filled the air with passes, and our wide receiver Juan Gutierrez who snatched most of them, and on the arresting play of our hard-hitting middle linebacker Mark Steenbergh who made many key tackles, we barely mustered a cordial "Thanks." Instead of being tied for the conference lead, we rode the bus solidly entrenched in second place in a conference of eight teams. Three games later, we finished the season still in second place; five of our players made the All-Conference Team. Our quarterback and wide receiver led the conference in passing and receiving, and both ranked among the top ten in the nation's NAIA colleges and universities. The academic records of the five All-Conference athletes were outstanding, and the overall classroom work of most of the other players was not unimpressive.

As a football coach with a Ph.D. in literature, I learned to live with an uncomfortable adjustment in my status. After studying for a Ph.D. for no less than ten years as an undergraduate and graduate, after publishing a number of articles in appropriately obscure scholarly journals, after doing research and study on a postdoctoral fellowship, I felt (and even my mother-in-law agreed) that I had earned the right to be called "Doctor" Hanna. It took less than five minutes of the first practice to change my title to "Coach" Hanna, and the change applied to my presence on the field, off the field, and in the classroom. It felt odd to hear a student ask, "Coach Hanna, could you please summarize your explanation of what this Eliot dude meant by that 'Objective Correlative' stuff?"

There was one instance when a player called me "Doctor" Hanna, but the call was done indirectly. It happened during a tense night game against the Mennonite Bluejays of Tabor College. With the score 3–0 in Tabor's favor early in the fourth quarter, a defensive player from Tabor was hurt. A stretcher was needed to remove him from the field. Before the trainers placed the player on the stretcher, the public address announcer asked that if a doctor was present, he should report to the field at once. At that point, our jovial wide receiver, a superb and confident player who, as a junior, had aroused the interest of the New York Giants, left our scraggly huddle on the field, ran to the sidelines in the direction of the tense head coach and yelled at him, "Coach, send Hanna in; they're calling for a 'doctor.'" The head coach's declared moratorium on smiles twisted the player around and shot him back to the huddle. During the postgame meal at midnight, the head coach joked about the incident which, as he put it, "seems a lot funnier now that we pulled the game out." Moments later he kidded, "Dr.-Coach Hanna, please pass the pepper."

This "name" business has been with me for a good while. In Oklahoma, many of my literary students felt that the S. S. Hanna sounded like a flagship, and at many of our editorial meetings for *Bananas*, they called me "Flagship." I learned to live with that name much as I had learned to live with "Coach" in Kansas. One football player, with whom I had shared my Oklahoma nickname, suggested a new name that evoked the ship and coach allusions. "A good nickname for you, coach," the player said, as I looked up at his goatee, "would really be 'Skip,' a name which—I might add in view of your imposing height—is *short* for Skipper."

Throughout the practice sessions, good, clean humor spun off the players' lips like twisting, turning, digging, flashy halfbacks spin off unsure tacklers. One day, for example, I scolded a tackler for failing to bring down a slow, lumbering linebacker who had intercepted a pass. "Hug him, hold on to him, and bring him down to the turf," I shouted. Then I asked, "How in the world could you miss hugging that guy?" To that, the player, a courteous and muscular lad from Tennessee, drawled, "Well, Coach Hanna, to tell you the truth, I don't know; maybe I thought Anita Bryant was watching."

From that incident, the English teacher in me learned a lesson in the connotation of words. The word the player was used to hearing was "tackling" a runner. "Hugging" another athlete, especially for some evangelical Christians who detested the ways of the homosexuals, carried uncomfortable connotations.

Many other players often exhibited a sense of irony and wit. Our star quarterback, for example, frequently complimented his receivers when they made extraordinary catches—catches that the radio announcers would call "incredible" or "spectacular"—by saying, "That was above average." If a receiver dropped a pass that hit his hands or punched the numbers on his jersey, the quarterback—mindful of the team's often heralded motto of 101 percent effort at all times—would moan, "Now, that's what you call a one hundred and *one* percent drop."

Occasionally, I found myself the butt of a joke. One player, for instance, asked me during a moment of levity in practice, "Coach Hanna, what's that on your helmet?" I reached up and brushed a blade of grass that was stabbed into the slight halo of my otherwise bald head.

To that little college on the flat lands of Kansas, the football program brought an enriching dimension in the presence of black student-athletes; it also brought students with Catholic, Greek Orthodox, or nonreligious backgrounds from distant states among them New York, Michigan, Tennessee, California, Florida, Alabama, Virginia, and Pennsylvania. Such students added plurality of viewpoints to a campus peopled and governed by the learned Presbyterians of the plains, a plurality that most faculty members and coaches welcomed and enjoyed.

Coexisting in that plurality often irritated certain players. One afternoon a devout Catholic player from Michigan came to my office and complained to me about the crusading ways of a player from the Assemblies of God denomination. "Coach Hanna," the player said, "Bob is a nice guy and he really knows his Holy Bible, but I'm a Christian, a Catholic; I was baptized as a baby, but he wants me to have a Charismatic believer's baptism as an adult, and he's so, so persistent, and I don't want to be rude to him. What do you think I should do?"

"First of all, please have a seat," I told the player.

"Thanks, coach," he said, as he sat on a wooden chair in the book-panelled office; he placed his notebook and a baseball cap that advertised a bar in Detroit on the corner of my cluttered desk.

Rocking in a swivel chair, I said, "I'll give you a suggestion that you might consider."

"Ok."

"Ask him to look at our religious denominations not as part of a melting pot, but as part of a stew pot, with potatoes, celery, carrots, meat, gravey, peas, etc."

"Ok, I've got that much."

"Then tell him that each Christian denomination is part of the pot, each has its distinctive features and flavor. Your point would be that denominational pluralism is a healthy part of our Christian framework," I stated.

"But chef—I mean coach—Hanna, the old boy won't be satisfied with that answer."

"How would he respond?"

"Oh, he'll probably say that the stew analogy is a good one—you know how he loves to eat—but he'll quickly make the Assemblies of God the meat in the pot."

"And the Catholics?"

"Oh, they might be the peas even though for centuries

before the Reformation his ancestors were Catholic."

"Argue back," I advised the player,"but do it lovingly, remembering all along that our faith consists of a personal relationship with Jesus Christ, one that transcends our petty denominational bickering."

"If I do, he'll start quoting Bible verses in response, and believe me, coach, he's good at that."

"Pray together, for that'll help you feel that urgent sense of Christian love."

"We tried that once."

"How did it go?" I asked.

"So, so, I'd say."

"Could you be more specific."

"Well, yeah, during the prayer he began to preach to me. In fact, a couple of times I lifted my head up to see whether he was preaching to me or praying to God."

"And—"

"And his head was lowered and eyes shut, but he was still preaching, coach."

"Charismatics," I assured the player, "have a tendency to reach out aggressively with their faith, but they really mean well. As a Baptist, I disagree with the Charismatics on a few issues, but in many ways they're the salt of the earth."

"Yeah, but salt is supposed to season and flavor. Isn't it, coach?"

"It sure is. The old adage says it best: 'Kissing a man without a mustache is like eating an egg without salt,'" I said, as my index finger and thumb pinched the edges of my mustache.

"But with him, coach, salt doesn't season; it smothers; he comes on way too strong. A thick layer of salt on a hamburger ruins it. Don't you agree?"

"I agree, but what can you do? You guys are teammates, and you've got to get along."

"I know, I know," the player said, as his right hand stroked a row of books.

"Perhaps—"

"Perhaps I can't do much. I really respect his tremendous football ability, but I feel so uneasy with his crusade to baptize me into their tradition."

"Is he that way with other non-Charismatics on the team?"

"With some he is, especially with those he calls 'nominal Catholics,' much like he was before he converted and later experienced the baptism of the Holy Spirit."

"How do they handle him?"

"A little abruptly, rudely," he said, as he looked at the dirty carpet in my office. He picked up a copy of *Christianity Today* from the pile on the side of the desk, flipped through it, and added, "I don't know, coach, I've been seriously thinking about these different denominations and the fact that they subscribe to the same creed, the—" He stopped speaking and listened. "What's that?" he asked, tilting his head toward the wall.

"Oh, they're probably falling pebbles," I said, "I've got a rat or two between these magnificent nineteenth century stone walls of Cooper Memorial and this dull and sickening twentieth century paneling. Don't let them bother you."

"But they do, they do," he said and stood. He put his cap on his head, clutched his notebook, and asked, "Coach, the Charismatics and the Catholics and the Methodists and the Presbyterians and the other well-known denominations all subscribe to the Apostles' Creed, don't they?"

"I believe they do."

"If that's the case, and in keeping with the position I play and the first job that I'll probably get, maybe I should go along with him."

"Let me see if I understand you correctly: you mean you're thinking of getting baptized as a Charismatic in the Assemblies of God tradition?"

"That's just what I'm thinking."

"And that would be above and beyond your Catholic baptism?"

"Just beyond, coach."

"Well—"

"Well, coach," he responded, as he began to leave, "I really want to get to heaven, and sometimes I think that even in religion, it might be wise for one to get double coverage." He reached over, shook my hand, squeezed it with authority, and smiled, as he said, "Bye, coach, see you at practice."

Another football player, one who pumped so much iron that his body appeared to be sprouting tumors, frequently entertained the class by dancing around risqué language. One day, for example, I lectured on euphemisms and asked, "What are the common euphemisms that we use for old people?"

"Senior citizens," one student said.

"Senior saints," another added.

"Golden agers," a third offered.

"Silver threads," a fourth noted.

"Explain what you mean by that," someone said.

"It refers to gray hair," came a reply.

"Any more?" I asked, paused, looked around the room, then added, "In the compositions that you write, you should avoid using euphemisms; occasionally you might get away with one: calling a 'Junk Yard' an 'Organ Donor Lot' might be an example of—"

"Wait a minute, coach, wait *a* minute," said the muscular football player who always wore in class a baseball cap advertising a Kansas Buick dealer. "Let me see if I hear you correctly: You don't want to see us use any of these euphemisms for old people? Is that right?"

"That's right," I said.

"So, what you want us to do is call old people by what they really are?"

"That's correct; I want your language to be honest and direct."

"In other words, we should refer to old people as 'old blank'?" After a slight pause, he said, "The censored word rhymes with parts."

The class roared, and I suspect they did so for at least two reasons: one, the player's somewhat Socratic technique clearly embarrassed me in more ways than one; and two, my quick smile at the player's remark must have assured the students that I had successfully resisted the impulse to lash out with a stern lecture on semantic morality.

Many football players kidded me in class, and they felt free to do so partly because they knew me in a coaching-teaching context, a context less intimidating than that often assumed by the learned, pompous brass behind the podium. My students' kidding occasionally knifed in truths that hurt. One day when I passed out evaluation forms to be used in assessing my performance as a freshman composition teacher, a player asked outloud, "Coach Hanna, would you drop our highest grade if we're honest?" Another player added, "How does one evaluate Dullesville?" A third said, "Since it's around Thanksgiving, we can say, 'a turkey of a prof.'" At the end of the class, I took a quick look at the evaluations, and I noted that most had placed me in the average or below average categories. A few gave me an excellent rating. Some wrote anonymous comments on the back of the evaluation blanks; most of the serious comments encouraged me to strive for better organization in the course; some advised me to do less testing, less lecturing, and concentrate more on discussion; others urged me to return the papers more quickly, or better yet, to assign fewer papers; several implored me to grade less harshly; one comment that stuck in my mind like a fly on a suicide strip simply stated: "I wish I could say, 'Write on Course with the S. S. Hanna,' but I can't."

In contrast to my classes, the head football coach ran "a tight ship." Strict rules governed Sterling College's football program. If a player violated the rules, he was disciplined accordingly. When our high-scoring kicker, a Greek Orthodox from Florida, missed several practice sessions without a valid reason, the head coach—having disciplined the player for another matter earlier in the season—asked him to leave the squad. His absence cost us what might have been a critical victory. But then the coach put his love for Christian principles above his lust for points on the board; this approach put him in high esteem with the community, the college, and the team.

Those principles, along with God's plan for salvation and the Christian life that comes with salvation, were often explored in our Monday afternoon devotions; they were also pursued in the Monday evening gatherings of the Fellowship of Christian Athletes sponsored by the head coach and open to all the college's athletes; they were preached in the Thursday sermons after practice by the team's chaplain. Before introducing the chaplain in those Thursday sessions, the coach always gave a thoughtful sermonette in which he used football imagery and related that imagery to life. The sermonettes and indeed the general crusade of the head coach led a once-born athlete from Detroit to remark in a small group discussion, "It's like this guys, to us Coach [Sam] Sample is like Paul, and to him we're the Corinthians."

Besides teaching and coaching in Kansas, I helped my students establish and publish issues of the *Great Plains Review*, a "Little" magazine in the tradition of Shawnee's *Bananas* and Bloomington's *Cantaloupe*. We called our prairie press "The Carpenter's Press" and used a plane for a logo. While I was in Kansas, Woodhix Press of Seattle, Washington, published a chapbook of my poetry under a strange title. In terms of sales, the chapbook became a spectacular and unequivocal failure. The publisher had hoped that reviews would help sales, but the work was reviewed in only one forum: *World Literature Today* of the University of Oklahoma. The publisher, searching for ways to increase sales, directed me to "write under a pseudonym a feature article on our peculiar quest for that strange title, noting especially the title's football connection." I did, and the feature was published in a widely circulating forum. Entitled "Cosell Inspires Cockroaches," the entire feature stated:

> Finding titles for books is far more difficult than finding names or titles for dogs, cats, or British dignitaries. Most editors and writers agree with this tidbit. The experiences of S. S. Hanna, a Ph.D. and a writer who teaches English and coaches football in Sterling College in Kansas, elevates this observation from a tidbit to a truth.
>
> One day, when a dirty, homeless, one-eyed, short-haired mutt followed him home, Hanna fed it and later begged

his wife to consent to the idea of keeping the dog. She
agreed, provided Hanna pledged to take the dog—daily—
to the campus and allow it to roam at will. Many of the
five hundred students at the college knew the dog, and
they detested it. Aware of that, Hanna trained the dog to
jump on people, and he promptly named it "Getlost."

"That name was easy to come by," Hanna recalls, "it
was calculated to control not the students' sentiments but
their vocabulary. I always chuckle," Hanna adds, "when-
ever I see the dog run up to a student who would instinc-
tively react by shouting 'get lost, get lost,' only to see the
dog leap up with tail-waving delight."

Similarly, when a stray cat found comfort in the di-
lapidated wooden structure that forms the back porch of
their house, the Hannas started to feed the dark, furry,
forever-purring little animal. It took little imagination or
time to come up with the name "Blackie."

Like the names of cats and dogs, the titles of British
dignitaries, Hanna believes, are easy to come by, for tradition and status dictate those titles. The titles of books,
however, are dictated by the sales potential they bring to
the book. For a book to sell well—the dream of every writer
and publisher—it must have a clever, memorable, strik-
ing, if not stirring, title. This lesson Hanna learned the
hard way.

Following the advice of a friend familiar with the publishing world, Hanna submitted a collection of his poems
to the Woodhix Press in Seattle, Washington, a small press
that concentrates on publishing poetry and graphics. "The
people at Woodhix really liked the poems," Hanna re-
members; "they even commissioned some excellent
graphics for the chapbook, but they insisted on getting a
catchy title before going to press."

For six weeks Hanna barraged Harvey Pigula, his editor at Woodhix, with title after title. All were rejected for
being "too bland and academic." One day, however, Pigula tentatively accepted a title that grew out of the imagery in one of the poems. The title read, "Where the Land
Has Muscle Tone: Poems from Kansas."

At Woodhix, that title endured for several weeks. It
was replaced by another title that grew out of another
poem. It read, "Feather in the Weather: Poems with a Light
Touch." This title also endured for several weeks, only

to be replaced by yet another title suggested by another poem. The title read, "Mirrors, Clones, and the Pill."

"For weeks," Hanna said, "the Woodhix folks would sleep on a title, but as press time neared, they'd change their minds." Hanna, who has written for the Literary Review, Symposium, Collier's Encyclopedia, the Texas Quarterly (forthcoming), and numerous other forums, believes that "to writers, delays in publication are infinitely more frustrating than rejection slips."

Finally, a most serious incident put to rest Woodhix's uncertainty. It happened during a cold and windy Monday night on the prairies of central Kansas. Hanna and his wife were in the family room of their two-story frame house. She was reading and he was watching a televised football game, a tense, spectacular aerial duel. Near the end of the second quarter, a cockroach cruised the top of the television set, crawled up the bookshelves, and cowered behind the books.

Hanna ignored the cockroach. "A navigating cockroach has never bothered me," he said. "When I was a single professor teaching at a university in Oklahoma, I lived in an apartment that had so many cockroaches that I nicknamed the place Roach Hall. After I got married, however," he added, "my wife, who is a registered nurse, developed in me what you might call 'cockrowiphobia,' that is the fear of cockroaches in the presence of a wife."

When his wife noticed the cockroach, she reacted. Following her orders, Hanna scrambled after the cockroach. He pushed some books, kicked others, shook the shelves, hoping all along to get the cockroach moving again. Wearing those sharply pointed cowboy boots, the kind that could trap and murder a cockroach in a corner, Hanna maintained his pursuit for several minutes. Frustrated in his failure, yet eager to watch the close game, he requested permission to carry out his search and destroy mission at halftime. His wife denied the request.

"If you want to be that way about it," Hanna fired back, "then turn off that light that you're reading by. If I'm not allowed to watch my game, then you shouldn't be permitted to read your book." After a long pause, he added, "Besides, this thing might be an albino cockroach. They glow in the dark, you know."

"Hey, there's your title," his wife said, "*Albino Cock-*

*roaches.* And if I were you, I'd forget about a subtitle. What you should do, instead, is write a catchy dedication to the book."

"Great idea," Hanna said, "I'll dedicate it to you and do it in a manner that expresses your presence in my life and the life of our Rita and Sal. The dedication, as I envision it, could become a national slogan for Notre Dame, and yet it could be an earnest expression from us to you: 'our lady.'"

"What would that dedication say?"

"It would simply say, 'To M. H. There is a bit of Notre Dame in all of us.'"

"Interesting," she said, "very interesting." She paused, reflected, then added, "I tell you, why don't you leave me out of the book and dedicate it to that fellow on the screen right now." She pointed to Howard Cosell who had just started his halftime Cosellisms. "Why listen to him," she said, "he's a marvelous commentator, a first-class word jock."

And so, the book went to the presses at last, and it rolled off the presses with the *Albino Cockroaches* title, and with a dedication that read:

> To Howard Cosell,
> The nation's #1 word jock.

The Woodhix people were overjoyed with the title and the dedication. So was Hanna. His wife, however, was disappointed with the final choices. After sleeping on them, she assured him that "few people would want your cockroaches around, even if they were protected by the Endangered Species Act. And that dedication, though a compliment of sorts, might just anger Howard Cosell."

"If it does," the professor of English replied with a wink, "wouldn't that be a nice piece of poetic justice?"

The feature article helped bring in orders from a number of quality places such as the Brown University Library, but the publisher still moaned, "We're like candidates for public office; we need quantity not quality." Even with the Cosell connection, *Albino* soared to a merited oblivion. Alice-Catherine Carls, an adjunct professor at Sterling, a brilliant and creative scholar who held a Sorbonne Ph.D., tried to change *Albino*'s course by helping me arrange a triple-hitter of an event: a collegewide, townwide, countywide poetry reading. Over one hundred bodies attended the reading, but few bought copies. Clara M. Belden, a gifted writer and teacher, wrote a clever feature on *Albino* for *Ye Sterling Stir*, but that too failed to stimulate sales. *Albino*'s firm, nonnegotiable failure led me to cancel its projected sequel: *Pointed Boots*.

One semester, in a Creative Writing class, we discussed an article from the *Writer* magazine that dealt with the importance of having good, arresting titles for books, poems, or stories. The discussion prompted me to tell the students all about *Albino Cockroaches* and "Termites in a Yo-Yo," that unpublished comic story of mine that had been going out and coming back with disturbing faithfulness. "Well, coach," a student said, "if you want your titles to get attention, they sure do; and if you'll forgive the cliché," he added, "they're cute as a bug."

Cute or otherwise, the titles or sales of chapbooks mattered to my future at Sterling far less than the enrollment of students. The dean of the college urged us to do all that we could to retain our students at a time when competition for students was extremely keen. The dean encouraged us to invite students for dinner and fellowship, to visit and counsel with them freely and frequently, to pay especial attention to issues that might matter to the students, even though those same issues might appear trivial to us as faculty.

At the end of my fourth year at Sterling, the collective effort of the faculty to retain our Sterling students and the efforts of the admissions officers to recruit many new ones failed somewhat, for enrollment dipped below the five hundred mark. The feisty college—not quite a century old, but determined to live on—made plans to declare in court a financial crisis in order to be able to terminate appointments of professors with tenure. Being the lowest jock-prof on the totem pole, I was without tenure, but I was good at sensing my impending demise and at writing letters and tucking in vitas in quest of teaching positions.

To my wife and me, the thought of leaving Kansas was

particularly painful, for we had spent four happy years on the prairies, highlighted by the birth of our Rita and Sal; by countless hours at farm and estate auctions that led us to furnish a house with unique and antique items; by my regular work as a lay speaker in small rural churches in central Kansas, churches that could not afford a full-time pastor; and by my football coaching responsibilities.

One evening, several football players came over to the house and gave me a going away present that consisted of two framed items: a picture of the team and another clipped from the *Milwaukee Journal*. The yellowish *Journal* picture showed a young man in old fashion football boots about to kick a tilted ball; next to it was a feature article that labeled the kicker's style as being, not soccer style, not straight ahead style, "but unorthodox, like a kid taking a swipe at a tin can." I was the subject of that feature, and when I had posed for the *Journal* photographer, I did it without wearing my football helmet; at the time, my head typified that of an eighteen-year old lad in the early sixties: it was full of hair. The Sterling Warriors knew me as the bald coach, the one whose head, from the back at least, resembled an egg fried sunny-side up. I appreciated the students' thoughtfulness and resourcefulness in researching and obtaining the picture, and I found their fascination with the decline and fall of my hair to be a bit touching.

For a diary entry in early April I wrote:

> I went to the campus post office to mail a "Thank You" card to the players who had presented me with the football pictures and to check the mail. As usual, Getlost followed and saluted his designated trees. In the box, there was an application for a job. I completed and mailed it this afternoon, and now I'm hoping and praying it'll lead to another job. My *dream* job has me teaching English *and* coaching baseball, a job where I could apply my baseball experience and write a book about it. Sterling's drama department put on another superb show today.

That April application did indeed lead to another fine but

also small (1430 students at the time of my interview) liberal arts college in Virginia. Tenure, unfortunately, was not part of the college's rank system; all faculty members worked on one-year contracts. Since I had no football coaching responsibilities with this—the third—teaching job of my stuttering career, I simply taught my classes (fifteen credit hours a semester), attended all meetings, kept regular office hours, and went home to prepare more lectures and grade more papers. My family responsibilities and heavy class load left no time for research and writing. In Kansas, my wife and I made two kids in four years; in Virginia, we made two boys in one: twins. The birth of Paul and Sami led our family to rejoice with the Psalmist, "Lo, children are a heritage of the Lord."

Strangely enough, my chances of getting tenure during my third teaching job were much dimmer than they were when I had started the quest for that first job back in Bloomington, Indiana. Still, I refused to despair and change professions much as some of my graduate school buddies had done. My renewed quest for a tenure-track appointment led me to search for yet another position, to type out letters and tuck in vitas. In time, Geneva College in Beaver Falls, Pennsylvania, picked me up from the waiver list of academe. Geneva is an old Reformed Presbyterian college with 1200 students, located in a working-class town of fourteen thousand people. The college featured a small but beautiful campus on a hill overlooking the Beaver River, a campus with large trees, stone buildings, stained glass windows, and flower studded grounds, a campus with traditions, towers, tennis courts, and the stadium where Joe Namath played his high school football.

Geneva, I learned during my interview, took great pride in being among the nation's few small liberal arts colleges that offered strong four-year degree programs in chemical, civil, electrical, industrial, and mechanical engineering. "Most colleges our size," the young and urbane librarian told me as he guided me through a tour of Geneva's superb library, "have a year or two of this or that engineering program, then a student has got to go elsewhere for the rest.

But we've got the entire package right here in Beaver Falls, and we've had it for over sixty years." Following a pause, he added, "But the college is much older than that, of course." Geneva, I also learned on that tour, "has a solid business program headed by a nationally known, well-published scholar who had served on several presidential commissions in the Nixon, Ford, and Carter years, and," the librarian continued as my eyes drifted to a colorful window that proclaimed the *Pro Christo et Patria* motto of the college, "we also have an excellent premedical program as indicated by our numerous and successful graduates in the medical field."

These programs and the traditional liberal arts offerings attracted a variety of bright students to Geneva. I expected to enjoy my stay with them, and I certainly did—until a crisis erupted, a crisis familiar to the gypsy scholars of the last quarter of the twentieth century. "The crisis," as one gypsy told me, "is rapidly becoming the anthem of our caste." What she had failed to tell me I often told myself while at Geneva, and that is: "My teaching and writing careers are charting not an 'upwardly mobile' but a 'downwardly stable' course, a perversely reassuring condition in the land of the Golden Tornadoes."

## CHAPTER FOUR
# Pennsylvania:
# Clouds of the Golden Tornadoes

As a writer who was moderately successful at failure, I sent out for editorial consideration several unpublished short stories, many unpublished poems, and six nonfiction pieces. I did this a month or so before driving up to Beaver Falls, Pennsylvania, and I did it with the realization that verdicts on some pieces should begin to come in when I arrive at Beaver Falls.

Word processors and xerox machines have made the commonly accepted practice of enclosing a self-addressed, stamped envelope (SASE) with short manuscripts a bit obsolete. These days, if editors refuse to return my rejected manuscripts at their own expense, I reason to myself, then let them shred them or shove them in their fireplaces; I'm tired of corresponding with myself. Moreover, all I'll need to do to get another copy of a given manuscript is xerox it again or pop the diskette into the machine and print. Either approach is cheaper than enclosing postage and envelopes for their return.

Sure enough, when I arrived in Beaver Falls, many of my manuscripts greeted me once again, but this time they were not in envelopes that I had bought, addressed, folded, licked, sealed, and stamped. Instead, they came in envelopes that had not been folded, carrying neat labels and metered postage. I felt at home in the Keystone state as I opened the envelopes, met my old friends, and read the rejection slips or the encouraging notes or the threats of never again returning scripts without SASE. An angry editor at IMAGE stuffed a sock with a rejected manuscript. The boots I always wore rendered matching socks superfluous, so I added the sock to my eclectic collection and the script to the "We're Back" file. Rejections took a decent turn: from slips to socks.

In Pennsylvania, all motor vehicles must display an official license plate only in the rear; the front could display all sorts of slogans. My first day in Beaver Falls, I saw a Datsun with a Pennsylvania plate in the rear and a front plate that read: "Buy American." I went to Geneva's bookstore during my second week, and there I noted all the paraphernalia advertising the school's nickname: GOLDEN TORNADOES. I bought a tornado license plate that consisted of a gold-colored human head contorted in such a way that its pate resembled a swirling frisbee, its eyes flashed a wrenchingly mean smile, its chin reached out and dangled like the trunk of an elephant. Sketched on a black background, the gold logo featured white strokes on the ears, eyes, and nose. The words GOLDEN TORNADOES, lettered in a banana pattern, framed the right side of the logo. Below the logo were the words: GENEVA COLLEGE, Beaver Falls, Pennsylvania. A colleague told me that a tornado once hit the tower of Old Main, a charming, century-old sandstone building, but it did little damage. Hence the paradox that forms the name.

"I see you've already got your brownie points," a personable administrator with a graduate degree from Harvard told me while pointing at the Geneva plate.

"Not exactly," I replied, "I just love the classy paradox implicit in the name."

"You know," he said, "that's the nicest thing I've heard anyone say about that name; we get all sorts of mail from alumni chiding us for changing our nickname to the Golden Tornadoes."

"What was it before that?" I asked.

"We were the Covies, short for Covenanters, the name of the Reformed Presbyterian denomination that founded and still governs the college."

That denomination, I later learned, traces its lineage to the original Presbyterians of Scotland, and it is often referred to as the Church of the Covenanters. The denomination's official name is the Reformed Presbyterian Church of North America. Its members are "Reformed" because they adhere to the principles set down by the Protestant Reformation of the sixteenth century. Their spiritual fathers include Martin Luther, John Calvin, and John Knox. They are called "Presbyterian" because of their form of church government, which consists of each congregation electing a group of elders who oversee the work of a given church and serve as part of the higher courts known as presbyteries and synods. Their covenanter label comes from their identification with public covenanting in Scotland, an act of protest in behalf of Christ's crown rights over the state and the recognition of Christ as king over the church without interference from the government. In 1743 the first Reformed Presbyterian congregation was organized in North America. In this country too, the kingship of Christ has been maintained as a foundational principle. The denomination played an active role in the Underground Railroad movement of the nineteenth century. It established its only seminary in 1810 and its only college in 1848: Geneva.

One of the earliest notes that I had received in my campus mailbox came from Geneva's head football coach. He had heard that I once played and coached football and wondered if I would be interested in joining his staff. I went to the gym, thanked the handsome coach for the invitation, and suggested that perhaps I could help at another season. I had hoped to spend my first year in Geneva adjusting to the setting, searching for appropriate housing, preparing for courses that I had not taught. While in the gym, I loitered and read the wall posters proclaiming the various records held by different players from Geneva's past. I examined the large display case with its new and tarnished trophies, its weathered and deflated footballs on which were painted the scores of memorable games, its certificates and pictures of all-American Covies and Golden Tornadoes.

While leaving the gym, I felt impressed by Geneva's past victories over current national powers among them the University of Pittsburgh and by the spectacular achievement of one of her sons, Cal Hubbard, who became the only man in American history to be enshrined in the College Football Hall of Fame, the Pro Football Hall of Fame, and the Baseball Hall of Fame. What impressed me most, however, was a framed yellowish sports page from a local newspaper that reported via a banner headline GENEVA BEATS HARVARD 16–7. The report spoke eloquently of the 1926 Covenanter squad as it traveled up to Cambridge, Massachusetts, and before a stunned crowd of twenty-five thousand upset the highly regarded men of Harvard and rode back in a train that might have well been labeled "The Covenanter Clipper." "When our Covies trimmed the Harvard Crimson," an old-timer told me, "football was a big thing at Harvard; they were a national power then, and we didn't have this 'Golden Tornadoes' business. If anything, we were simply 'The Tornadoes.' "

Geneva's student body—unlike that of some evangelical colleges where the students are required to be born-again Christians and to be recommended by their pastors—consists of students with different religious backgrounds. In my classes, for example, some students were Jewish, Muslims, or agnostics; others were Greek Orthodox, Mennonites, Episcopalians. Geneva even had a Buddhist student. A survey that was conducted by the college showed that Catholics formed the second largest Christian denomination at Geneva. "For years," I was told by an established colleague, "Catholics formed the largest denomination on campus, and that's due partly to the high number of Catholics in the Western Pennsylvania region where most of our students come from, and it is also due to the excellent relationship that the college enjoys with its Catholic students and friends."

"The many Catholics and the few Muslims and Jews,"

another faculty member told me, "add a healthy measure of pluralism to Geneva, a pluralism with which many evangelical colleges might feel uneasy."

"Do the Muslims and the Jews," I asked, "feel uneasy about attending chapel?"

"I suppose some do," he replied and began to explain Geneva's chapel system.

Chapels are held three times a week, but students are required to attend only ten chapels a semester. The speakers and their topics are announced at the beginning of each semester, and many of the topics deal with such significant issues of the human condition as world hunger; the nuclear freeze and God's people; abortion; justice and the Blacks' struggles in contemporary America. The differing rays of the Christian spectrum are presented on most issues. On the nuclear freeze issue, for example, peace through strength proponents, just-war advocates, and Anabaptist pacifists would be invited to speak at different times in a given year. Chapel also features occasional worship services with emphasis on such issues as the miracles of Jesus, the new birth experience, the Lordship of Christ.

"Given the variety of topics and speakers in chapel," one Jewish student told me, "I pick what appears interesting and simply go. I look at it this way: you don't have to believe everything you hear."

A Muslim put it a bit differently, "I go, and I often find myself debating my friends on what chapel presents. The name of the game is to integrate faith with discipline, isn't it?" he asked.

"That's right," I replied.

"So, I integrate, and I find myself coming at most issues from an Islamic perspective, one that gets me in trouble with my Christian friends many of whom have a hollow Hollywood knowledge of Islam."

Hollywood films form a central cultural experience at Geneva. Each semester a colleague of mine in the English department teaches a popular film course that brings to campus American and European film classics addressed to mature and sophisticated audiences. Students and faculty members and their families who are not enrolled in the class for credit pay a small fee and join the class to view a given film. Student groups in dorms or organized clubs often compete with my colleague's plans by renting their own films and showing them for small fees. Film rentals at Geneva, like bake sales elsewhere, serve as good money-making devices for all sorts of organizations.

One day, the parents of a prospective student who were touring the campus and who had stopped in my office for a brief visit told me that the students' interest in films, the lack of a dress code at Geneva, the light chapel requirement, the religious pluralism on campus, the occasional display of personal affection that they had seen in the dorm and student lounges—all formed what one parent labeled as "clear signs of creeping liberalism." The liberalism charge and the disdainful tone in which it was offered led me to respond with a mini sermon on religious life at Geneva.

"We do," I said, "have several 'don'ts' (no drinking, no dancing, to mention two examples), but to call Geneva liberal or about to cave into liberalism is ill-advised." I went on to defend Geneva by saying that "on the fundamentals of the faith, Geneva's administration and faculty are every bit as conservative as most evangelical schools. All the Geneva scholars who I know believe in the authority of the Scriptures, the Virgin birth, the resurrection of our Lord, the Second Coming, and so on. If anything, Geneva keeps the Sabbath holy, and the Covenanters do it with more reverence and care than any other Christian group that I know. Most Covenanter students and faculty members refuse to even watch television on the Sabbath; no one may use the college's tennis courts on the Sabbath; the Monday after a long holiday is always a day off at Geneva, and this is granted so that the students and their parents are not forced to travel on the Sabbath."

The uneasy parents who had driven on the Sabbath for a Monday visit of the college seemed unimpressed, so I continued, "Bible study groups meet in all the dorms; they're not required, but students who want them organize them, and numerous students from different denominations attend them. We even have small group Bible studies among the faculty. The Christian students support each other and influence the non-Christians by their examples. The bookstore stocks classics in books from the secular and Christian worlds; the campus radio station has a nice balance between secular and Christian music; the students' dating life is not as heavily regulated here as at, say, Bob Jones University. Let me tell you," I concluded my little sermon by saying, "there's plenty of piety and prayer and Bible study at Geneva."

In time, I learned that there was something "more" to the Geneva spiritual experience. I met, for example, a group of students whose religious convictions impinged on an important contemporary issue: world hunger. The students organized themselves into a group and tried hard to rally other students to support their cause. Every week, the group members prayed and fasted by giving up their Wednesday evening dinner meal. The food services assigned a certain dollar amount for each missed meal; the money collected was then given to organizations involved in alleviating world hunger.

"Wouldn't that be great," one philosophy student in the group told me as we sat in a booth in the Brig, the snack bar in the Student Center, "if our actions influence others to such an extent that Kant's Categorical Imperative begins to take hold in this matter."

"He can talk about Kant," another student added, "but I'll stay with Peter, Paul, and Jesus."

"It is precisely Jesus," the philosophy student responded, "who charges us to use our faith as an entrance into the harsh and demanding realities of a world of hurt, but rather than do that, too many of us use our faith as an exit, as an escape from those brutal realities. Prayer offers us the illusion of having done something to alleviate the unbearable suffering of mankind. And prophecy, or our simplistic understanding of it, lead us to question what can be done. We often justify our inaction with resort to Bible verses such as 'There will be wars and rumors of wars,' or 'The poor are forever with us.' But such verses obstruct our view of the sweep of the Biblical teachings on compassion and peace."

"Please elaborate," I suggested to the student, "on your exit-entrance distinction."

"That's easy," he replied. "To read the Bible and pray every day is not enough; those who do just that form your classic 'exit Christians.' One must get involved, meshed into the brutalities of life."

I pressed him for another illustration from the ways of an "entrance Christian," assuming his group's fasting, world-hunger project to be such an illustration. He responded quickly: "Take, for example, the faculty members and students who spent last summer in Haiti building schools, churches, and other projects. These people aren't missionaries, but they are Christians doing missionary work; and I believe every Christian, if he's to be a Christian, must realize the dictates of the great commission, and that means to go out into the world and do—and I really mean do—the Lord's work. It's that simple. Like you always tell us in class," the student added by alluding to one of my clichés, " 'You learn to write by doing'; so too, you serve the Lord Jesus Christ by doing; the Christian life is a demanding life, a difficult life, and that's why the world has so few authentic Christians."

Beyond sharing with me their admirable Christian commitment, many of my Geneva students often poked genial fun at my copious limitations. One day, for example, I alerted my American Literature class, "Next Tuesday you'll have an unannounced quiz on Melville's 'Billy Budd,' so make sure you read it." Then I spoke about wit and the simile. To illustrate my point, I told the students of an incident involving my four kids, their poodle, and a swimming pool. "The kids stood in the backyard pool and splashed water on each other," I said, "and their blondish poodle, Muff, paced the area, fanning his tail, whining and pleading for attention. So, one of the kids reached over, grabbed Muff, and asked, 'Should I dunk him?' The other kids shouted 'Yea' and clapped and screamed as little Muff went under.

He kicked and kicked and scurried out of the pool. His once fluffy blond hair, now soaked, matted itself on his long, thin body; the site of a wet Muff led one of the boys to observe, 'Hey, everybody, look at Muff, he looks like a French fry.' " The students smiled and I continued the lecture, "A simile of this sort has a kind of—"

"Forget about lecturing on similes, Doc," one student said, "and tell us more of your kids' stories; they're funnier than those grownup tales you come up with."

In another class I once quoted that passage from Proverbs that proclaims, "A merry heart doeth good like a medicine; but a broken spirit drieth the bones." In response, a football player—who always wore a baseball cap that converted his head into a billboard—said, "I know your merry heart doeth good like a medicine, but your classroom lectures, oh those lectures—well, to put it simply and truthfully, they're dry as bones." He paraphrased the proverb to suit the occasion. That day I had lectured on the intricacies of Dante's *Purgatorio*, not exactly one of those popcorn topics that invade and engage the jocks' attention. Near the end of the lecture when I had brilliantly succeeded in reducing the number of eyelashes in class, I asked: "All those who believe that Dante is the first name of the Florentine poet please stand." The entire class stood, and I kidded them by saying, "This should remind you of the seventh inning stretch," and to that, one replied, "Yep, but what a boring ball game."

I'll admit that my lectures at Geneva scaled the heights of boredom much as they had done in my previous teaching ventures. And as I had done before, I tried to undermine boredom with humor. One of my classes met in a room that had a large clock on a side wall. The people sitting in the last four rows of the class could see the clock by simply glancing at it, but those seated in the first four rows had to turn around and look at it or focus it in their make-up mirrors. Most of my students, courteous as they were, refused to turn and look at the clock; to many of the football players in class, turning around would have been a penalty equivalent perhaps to roughing the passer or the kicker, a sort of an unsportsmanlike cheap shot. Whatever, in appre-

ciation of their courtesy, I often weaved into my lectures
remarks that pleased them; I would frequently say without
breaking stride: "And Dante in the *Purgatorio* argued for
the benefit of the people in the first four rows there are ten
minutes remaining that a person's sins. . . ." Some students would invariably find themselves writing "for the
benefit of . . ." then interrupt their note taking to salute
their boredom with a smile.

One day in the midst of a difficult and long grammar
test, one of my student-athletes raised his hand and I called
on him. Rather than ask a question or motion me to his
desk, he made an unusual remark. "Dr. Hanna," he said,
"this test is much too difficult; it's a pain in—well, let's
say—the coordinating conjunction."

When I collected the test, I gave a writing assignment
and spoke on the importance of practice in writing, the importance of learning by doing. "Practice is important," I said,
"in learning to swim, to play tennis, to type, to write." Then
I spoke about the time in college when I used to go into
the woods behind the fraternity house and practice deliv-
ering an assignment for speech class. "Why I would speak
and shout and gesture; I would exhort the trees, the bees,
the birds; and every once in a while, the squirrels would
gather, and I would speak to them too; I would continue to
go over the speech until—"

"I wonder," a student interrupted by saying, "what would
the squirrels say to each other as they heard you, Dr. Hanna?"

Before I could reply or even think of a reply, one student
deadpanned, "Just another nut."

After that class, a student suffering from a postexami-
nation hangover walked with me to my office. Making small
talk, he asked what I was working on in my fiction. I told
him that I was writing a comic novel that deals with the
life of Gladys Princeton and the men of Kansas Air. I mentioned that old lady Princeton was a shrewd eighty-three-
year-old widow, blessed with an ironic wit, and with wealth,
cynicism, piety, imagination, and spunk. I added that "I had
just completed a correspondence that Mrs. Princeton had
undertaken with the executives of four airlines about a

matter that is dear to the life of senior citizens."

As we walked, the student pressed me for details, and I continued, "The Gladys Princeton of my fiction was willing to give a huge financial donation to a commercial American carrier that would agree to divide the cabins of its aircraft into two clearly labeled sections: 'Constipated and Nonconstipated,' And you know what," I added with a big smile, "that lady came mighty close with one carrier. As the correspondence shows, the carrier's executives had agreed to her request, provided the signs were marked in a number code. Mrs. Princeton, however, insisted that the signs be clearly marked in English and Spanish and placed below the 'Fasten the Seat Belts' signs. (She gave in slightly, and I might add graciously, by agreeing to forgo the literacy graphics that usually accompany such signs). To this day, that carrier's jets fly both kinds of passengers, and they fly them unmarked."

"Are you poking fun at old people with that bit of fiction?" my student asked.

"Oh, no, no, not at all. My folks are old, and I love them dearly. What I'm doing is exactly the opposite: I'm trying to smash a stereotype of old people by showing that old people can be quite sagacious."

"Whatever that means," he added, as we climbed the stairs leading to my office.

"And I'm also trying to make a comment on contemporary culture, and I trust my distaste for big government comes through in the piece."

"Perhaps your next piece," my student, a farm boy from Missouri, said, "will take a different drift." He winked and began to talk about the examination.

At Geneva, all professors were free—indeed, they were invited—to integrate their Christian faith with their disciplines. Frequently, I used examples from the Bible by way of illustrating various literary devices such as simile, metaphor, overstatement, and paradox. I divided the class into small groups consisting of four or five students, and I asked each group to search the Bible for a given device. The students loved the exercise, and they often isolated an impressive array of examples, for many knew the Scriptures, and they quickly acquired a grasp of the characteristics of a given device.

In my lectures on irony, I usually asked the students to go beyond the Bible and offer examples from contemporary affairs before we launched into a study of the poems or stories in our text. During one session, a student charged out to another campus and asked, "Isn't it ironic that Oral Roberts has now built a huge hospital on his campus after all his spiritual healing emphasis?" A second student mentioned a television film on the life of Christ and then asked, "Wouldn't it have been ironic if after the manger scene a diaper commercial appeared, or if a dishwashing commercial appeared following the Last Supper scene?" I chuckled and then gave a mini lecture—stimulated by my reading of Elton Trueblood's brilliant little treatise on *The Humor of Christ*—on Christ's frequent, complex, and subtle use of irony in the Synoptic Gospels.

"In a school such as ours," a third student said, "we de-emphasize and denounce as sinful premarital and extra-marital sex—and rightly so. We even discourage students from swapping spit in public. Yet—and here's where the irony is—we employ a dean for student affairs."

One sunny fall afternoon, our English class met on the lawn in front of Old Main. There, I tried to illustrate the definition of allegory by using a poem from my Cafe Series. I distributed to the students a poem xeroxed from *Albino Cockroaches*, and I outlined the incident that had inspired it. Then I suggested that a network of images or references or symbols often informs an allegorical work. I asked the students to look for the system of contrasts in the poem entitled "At a Cafe in Madrid." I read:

> It doesn't take long
> for a bald man to realize
> that the rest of the world has hair,
> or for a short man
> that there is height somewhere.
>
> To a Spanish-speaking beggar

with a babe in arms,
'no comprendo'
is cruel as hair is dear to a bald,
short, rather puzzled millionaire.

The students saw the poem as an allegory on "the have and the have-nots," and they felt that the poem's contrasts—bald-hair, cruel-dear, poverty-plenty, short-height, puzzled-realize, beggar-millionaire—supported their view. "Your analysis is pretty much what I had in mind when I wrote that little poem," I said as I turned their attention to Laurence Perrine's discussion of allegory in his famous literature textbook. In my impending pursuits of tenure and publication, the students' analysis took on a special poignancy.

During another class session, our discussion somehow drifted to bumper sticker theology. Most of the students offered thoughtful and intelligent remarks criticizing the proclamation of serious spiritual truths from the bumpers of dirty and rusty cars. One student even pointed to the weak theology of some of those stickers; for an example, the student used the popular sticker that says, GOD SAID IT/ I BELIEVE IT/ THAT SETTLES IT. "Even on a brand new shining Cadillac, this is still bad theology," the angry student said, and added, "Who cares if you believe it or not? The truth is: God said it and that settles it."

"Speaking of bumper stickers," another student said, "my absolute favorite has got to be the one that I saw the other day on a philosopher's car. The sticker asked, HAVE YOU HUGGED YOUR PHILOSOPHER TODAY? A strange question indeed, for philosophers tend to be as huggable as porcupines."

The bumper sticker discussion led me to tell the students all about Car Couplet Inc., a small corporation started by an inventive character in my unpublished fiction. The character thinks up, designs, and markets literary-philosophic couplets that are to be used not as bumper stickers, but as "trunk thoughts," to be placed not on Fords or Chevys, but on Volvos and Mercedes; she advertises the couplets not in the *National Enquirer*, which is for inquiring minds, but in the *New Yorker* and *Harper's*. The couplets tend to be a bit longer than conventional bumper stickers, and they always tend to rhyme or make an attempt to do so. When the Geneva students pressed me for examples, I offered four from different categories. For a seminary professor from West Virginia who is turned-off by the crassness of bumper stickers, Car Couplet offers:

> Strip God off your bumper sticker
> Mine Him in your human ticker.

For those people who feel threatened by the barbaric promises of genetic engineering and their implications for ethical thought, there is a couplet that states:

> When birth by cloning works its will,
> The mirror will be our safest pill.

To a grandmother who drives a car with a bumper sticker that says ASK ME ABOUT MY GRANDCHILDREN but says nothing about her status as a mother-in-law, the Car Couplet outlet suggests a thought that hints on both concerns:

> Their mother is lovely, their father is pompous,
> Their children are gifted, thanks to Christmas and us.

"These couplets are wordy for bumper stickers, Dr. Hanna," one student said.

"But they're not exactly bumper stickers," I said in defense of my character, "they're trunk thoughts, a new genre on the American literary scene." Before leaving the trunk-thought topic, I recited one designed especially for those poets who feel that their profession is being devalued by the dogged doggerelists of the day:

> The true poet triggers and graphs and shows
> Goose bumps flowing like falling dominos.

At the end of that class session, I went to the Brig to while away an hour or so and to fortify myself for the next class by drinking a couple cups of coffee. Balancing a cup in my right hand, I walked up to an unoccupied booth, claimed it, and wrote a few notes for a short story idea that had occurred to me during the previous lecture-discussion session. I expected to write the story during the upcoming Christmas vacation. The notes stated:

The story might begin by introducing an erudite, nationally unknown counseling psychologist who drives a Volvo with this trunk thought:

If your problems float like dead flies in a stale drink,
Cheer up and head to the couch of your local shrink.

The story might well continue by developing the character of the psychologist as he delivers a series of lectures at a major seminary on the theme of inferiority and loneliness. A day after the psychologist leaves the campus, he receives a telephone call from the seminary's president who had chaperoned him throughout his extensive three-day visit to the campus. The call passes on this disturbing news: one of the students who had attended the lectures and who had confessed to being a great admirer of the psychologist committed suicide.

The psychologist instantly decides to drive back to the seminary for a memorial service. While driving, his car hits a pothole, resulting in a flat tire. He stops at a gas station to have it fixed. At the station, he stands and observes the repair work of a scruffy mechanic with a baseball cap, greasy clothes, dirt under his fingernails, and teeth that looked as if they've been cooked in curry. For small talk, the neatly dressed psychologist tells the mechanic all about the lecture series and the "tragic suicide." The mechanic listens as he pursues the routines of fixing a flat. When the mechanic pumps the tire with air, the psychologist completes the story, pays for the service, thanks the mechanic who, in turn, skips his usual "Righto" reply and asks instead: "What in the world did you say to trigger the suicide?"

That question holds hostage the psychologist's thoughts as he drives back to the memorial service. The drive gets longer and longer and the agony of intense thought gets more painful and poignant as the psychologist yearns for the company of others with whom to share his thoughts. Those thoughts should illuminate and focus the story's main theme.

After sketching the story's contours, I returned to the Brig's snack shop for a second cup of coffee. I walked up to a booth where a student of mine was sitting and I said, "May I join you?"

"Change that to a declarative sentence," he said.

"I just joined you, man."

"Good."

"Boy, this mint tea is fine," he said, "I just love tea after tea."

"You know that's an old British Pub expression, don't you?"

"What expression?" He asked.

"Tea after tea. Do you have an idea what it alludes to?"

"It alludes to liking a lot of tea, one cup of tea after another. It's tea conversation; it's not supposed to be deep," the student said.

I felt the student might enjoy the expression and he might use it more frequently if he knew its loaded connotation. "I'm really surprised you don't know what it alludes to," I said.

"Well, tell me, what does it mean? I'm really curious now."

"I tell you, the phrase has two meanings: one means that you do indeed like one cup of tea after another, but the second meaning is a bit more subtle; it alludes—in a manner of speaking—to cows."

"To what?"

"You heard me right—"

"Cows?"

"Yes, cows."

"But, Dr. Hanna, cows give milk, and we're talking about tea."

"I know we're talking about tea."

"So, where's the connection?" the student asked.

"The connection is between the cow and the milk."

"Say that again."

"The connection is between the cow and the milk."

"Come on, Doc, come on, you're making all this sound like a classified revelation of the prophet Muhammad."

"That can't be," I said, "with Muhammad we associate camels, and we're talking about cows."

"Cows, cows," the student repeated, pensively.

I yanked a pen out of my shirt pocket and diagrammed a clue on the napkin next to my cup. The student laughed and winked his approval. "You're right about that, you're very right," he said.

Following that remark, a young man staggered to our booth, set a pile of books on the table, and went to the snack shop. "He's got as many books here as the rich and famous movie stars have bathrooms in a single house," I said.

When the young man returned to our booth with a cup of hot chocolate, he asked, an instant after he sat down, "May I join you?"

"Hanna is my name," I said, shook his hand, glanced at a young lady with mustard-colored hair that was full of artificial ingredients as she walked by our booth.

"I'd be very disappointed if that's not your name," the young man said, releasing his grip. "I sure hope I get good money for these books from that book buyer."

The three of us exchanged small talk, then I rose, excused myself, bought another cup of coffee, and in keeping with my habit, walked the sidewalks of Geneva's gorgeous campus, occasionally stopping to sip that hot, dark, legal, bitter, aromatic, addictive, mind-expanding, ever so tasty brew. I went to my office and wrote another test.

I began my second semester at Geneva College by assuming the position of advisor of the student newspaper, the yearbook, and the literary magazine. The weekly paper, the *Cabinet*, was edited by a bright and energetic young lady, inquisitive, kind, and articulate. The assistant editor, a center on the football team, wrote a regular column for the paper, a column that was frequently witty, provocative, and probing. The newspaper had enough of an investigative edge to prevent the renaissance of the *Liquor Cabinet*, a spirited underground Geneva tabloid.

At a dull moment during registration day for the second semester, the assistant editor came to the English desk at the gym and confided in me, "We just learned the name of our graduation speaker and that he'll be granted an honorary doctorate; the editor and I dislike that, and we plan to oppose him—vigorously." We made eye contact as he added, "We also learned that major faculty cuts, especially in the liberal arts areas, are coming this semester, and we plan to oppose those cuts. All I'm telling you," he concluded, as we once again made eye contact, "is that it promises to be a hot semester for you as advisor, a baptism that'll make you long for your days as a football coach in Kansas."

At a dinner discussion, the editors told me that the graduation speaker was a business executive whose highly visible company employees had a tendency to celebrate material gains; the editors felt that this concern—and there were others—clashed with Geneva's spiritual emphasis. They were careful to note that the executive should be permitted to address the student body at a convocation, "but graduation and the granting of an honorary doctorate," they argued, "are special occasions that might best be served by a speaker who does not engender so much controversy."

Many students and faculty members felt that the editors—well-intentioned and conservative Christians—overstated their case in opposing the executive. Several students defended the executive in letters to the editor and in guest columns in the *Cabinet*. The editors saw to it that the competing issues in this and other matters were presented systematically and fairly in the newspaper.

The graduation speaker controversy caught the faculty off guard. Some scholars began to observe, during coffee sessions at the Brig, that the students and not the faculty were leading the college on a crucial issue. So, a special faculty meeting was held, and a motion to rescind the invitation to the speaker was made. The Geneva president took the floor and spoke eloquently and cogently against the motion. He won the day, for the motion was discussed, analyzed, explained, dissected, amended, fleshed out, and—at the end of two hours—tabled. It never came off the table. Reason: the speaker apparently heard of the controversy generated by his acceptance of the Geneva invitation, and in the interest of an orderly and dignified graduation, he kindly offered to withdraw his acceptance. The Geneva president reluctantly accepted the offer and quickly located another speaker from nearby Pittsburgh.

Throughout the stormy incident, the president, who had selected the business executive and recommended him to the board of trustees for an honorary doctorate, conducted himself in an exemplary manner. At no time did he call me in and ask me to put an end to the editors' pursuit of the issues involved; the president had a healthy respect for a free and responsible press, and the editors involved conducted themselves in an aggressive but honorable manner. That incident had the potential of being a hot one for me, but it turned out to be lukewarm.

The faculty cutbacks, however, were another matter. The president, a strong leader who had the wisdom and the courage to make difficult decisions, took charge of the "cuts," as they came to be known, early in the second semester in the dead of winter. He announced to the entire college family his decision—supported by the board of trustees—to make a 15 percent reduction in faculty, administration, and staff; he planned to implement the cuts by the end of the academic year. The announcement sent ripples of discontent that later turned to waves of anger in most faculty and staff members, many of whom had expected a 5 percent cutback. Declining enrollment and demographic projections, carefully researched and assessed by the president, formed the basis for the cutbacks.

Tenured and untenured faculty members were eligible for

the cuts, though the tenured would be enticed by a number of voluntary severance packages. For about a month, faculty members speculated as to who might go voluntarily, who might better go voluntarily, who might take early retirement, who might be likely to find a job elsewhere, who might go into preaching full-time, and who might need to retool. My department had four full-time professors; all of us had Ph.D.s from excellent universities; all were tenured but me, and the tenured had a reputation for being outstanding teachers. So I expected to be cut, though several established colleagues in other departments kept telling me, "Don't bank on it; the situation is such that anyone could go." One faculty member put it more bluntly, "I bet you're the lowest paid fellow in the English department, and in these hard times, you must look pretty good to the president."

The *Cabinet* published several articles and editorials reporting and deploring the cutbacks. The editors feared that the liberal arts were going to be unfairly singled out for surgery while business and engineering—two of Geneva's strongest departments—would remain untouched. The president maintained that the cutbacks would be across the board in all areas and that they were necessary if the college were to make better use of its resources and to maintain its high academic standards, fiscal responsibility, decent wages, competitive tuition, and Christian stewardship.

Throughout the early weeks of that first winter in Pennsylvania, I felt some "heat"; it was generated, however, not by anything that the *Cabinet* editors had written or published, but by fear of being cut so soon from a school that I liked so much. That fear led me to compose a new curriculum vita and a cover letter to be used in search of yet another teaching position. Thanks to Geneva's generosity, I had in my office an excellent word processor and a printer; both eased the pains of my perennial correspondence; neither had the capacity to locate specific teaching vacancies.

I searched for such vacancies in the English sections of the *Chronicle of Higher Education*. I also consulted that forum's vacancy listings for academic deans, vice-presidents, and presidents, even though I had no interest whatsoever in administrative posts. Several friends with low-level administrative experience had asked me to nominate them "to posts that appear interesting." One fellow even assured me that if he became a high-level administrator, he would create at his new institution a tenure-track position to suit my credentials. "The old cliché," as he put it, "still holds true: 'It's not what—but who—you know that counts.'" In the next breath, he added, "Most of those jobs in the *Chronicle*, in my opinion at least, are nonjobs, placed there to comply with Affirmative Action guidelines, but let's see what comes up."

Moreover, I subscribed to the *Job Listing* of the Modern Language Association, a quarterly that prints most available positions in English. This quarterly, others like it in various disciplines, and the *Chronicle* will offer sociologists or historians interested in America's gypsy scholars a clear picture of the prevalence of temporary, nontenure-track teaching positions for the Ph.D.s of the last quarter of the twentieth century.

Conventional cover letters and curriculum vitas had helped me locate teaching, research, and coaching positions in several states. The tight job market for Ph.D.s in English had deteriorated since that year in Indiana when I began the search for my first teaching position. Aware of that, I felt that an unconventional vita might isolate my name from the slush pile of applicants for a given position. Accordingly, I wrote such a vita and patterned its title on that of an old movie. I had hoped that the vita's sense of humor would click with that of a search committee or a dean or a department head, leading me to a decent job. Just one job. That's all I needed.

To insure that the vita elicited attention, I sent an unconventional cover letter with it, a letter that consisted of a one-liner that asked: "Might this interest you, or do you recommend suicide?" I reasoned to myself: "If the vita fails to click into a job, the responses to it, to its cover letter, and to the peculiar picture that I plan to enclose might furnish me with materials for an article. The one and one-half page vita stated:

## THEY WRITE VITAS, DON'T THEY?

*PERSONAL*

| | |
|---|---|
| Name | S. S. HANNA. |
| Address | 3918 Peace Drive, Frictionville, Pa 15010. |
| Phone | Unlisted. |
| Health | Radioactive. |
| Height | Short. Growing shorter with age. |

*EDUCATION*

Ph.D. Yale University, 1972.
Recalled in the Summer of '82.
Dissertation Title: AN EXAMINATION OF THE PRES-
ENCE AND SYMBOLIC SIGNIFICANCE OF THE
CRACK IN THE DATE SEED AS USED IN A SELECT
NUMBER OF THE UNPUBLISHED AND POSITIVELY
OBSCURE POEMS OF THE EARLY TWELFTH CEN-
TURY POET BENEDICTO MORAVIA LAKABOZO OF
MILANO.

M.A. Balls State University, 1968 B.A. Parsons College
(The late Parsons College).

*EXPERIENCE*

Janitor-in-Residence: The Three Mile Island Nuclear Plant
(TMI).

Visiting Scholar: Held the John Dewey Chair in Education at Columbia University. Enclosed is a photograph to
that effect; it's dated the day I made the visit and held
the chair.

Editor-in-Chief: *Burpless*, a "Little" magazine graphing
the contours of the literary sensibility in contemporary
American culture. *Burpless* is now dead.

*PUBLICATIONS*

Wrote many things, published nothing. (I'm an unknown
writer, waiting to be discovered). Work in progress: *The
Plastic Surgeon Whose Nose Fell Off* (a comic novel).

*HONORS*

Winner of the Best Tenured-Teacher-of-Dated Knowledge
Award, academic year 1980–'81. WHO's WHO? (He's
Chairman of the Board at Sony's main office in Tokyo).

*PATENTS*

Holds a patent on Proflow/3, a new improved laxative designed especially for the convenience of full professors.

Dear Reader:

The above is done in allegorical fun. In all seriousness, if the following quick review of my credentials interests you, then please consider contacting me. My real name is that listed above, but my address, phone number, and credentials are these:

*English Department, Geneva College, Beaver Falls, Pa 15010 (412 Area Code 846 5100)*

Ph.D. Indiana University, 1973. Major: Literature. Postdoctoral work on a grant from the National Endowment for the Humanities, Amherst, Mass. Taught courses in American Literature, World Literature, Writing, and Journalism. Taught at four liberal arts colleges in Oklahoma, Kansas, Virginia, and Pennsylvania. Coached football (assistant), established and advised literary magazines in Oklahoma and Kansas. Published in numerous forums among them *Publishers Weekly*, the *Chronicle of Higher Education*, *Collier's Encyclopedia*, *Symposium*, *World Literature Today*, *Literature East and West*, *Twentieth-Century Literary Criticism* (the reference work), the *Wascana Review*.

"What would you do," a colleague asked me, "if in response to your one-line cover letter, you get a one-word response?"

"Well, that depends on the word, of course."

"Suppose you get a certain four-letter word—"

"There are lots of those."

"The one I have in mind begins with an 's,'" my colleague said, smiling.

"Oh."

"It's often used in colloquial English."

"Oh."

"It is often associated with negative odors, and I mean negative."

"I hear you," I said.

"That's good," he replied, "but it's not what you're thinking of."

"What is it then?"

"Sure." He smiled; the deodorant commercial buzzed my thoughts.

"Well, if the 'Sure' indicates an interest in my vita, that's great."

"Ah ha, but what if it responds to 'suicide,' after all that was part of the question, wasn't it?"

"It sure was, and I tell you—I'd cross that bridge when I get to it. Will I?" I asked, backtracking out of my colleague's office into mine.

A student who had come up to see me was already seated in my office. I sat down and apologized: "Sorry I'm a bit late; I was just talking to the chairperson—"

"Don't use that word," the student said, "I dislike it."

"Which word?" I asked.

"Chairperson."

"Why?"

"Because it's stupid."

"Stupid?"

"You bet it is."

"Explain what you mean," I said.

"Ok, you get rid of the word 'chairman' because 'man' at the end of that word suggests a male, then you put instead 'chairperson' and the word 'son' still suggests a male."

"You've got a good point there," I admitted, then added, "I guess we'll have to go back to saying 'caveman' instead of 'caveperson' and 'sportsmanship' instead of 'sportspersonship.' "

My attempts at humor failed, so I turned the conversation to his problems with my favorite author: Franz Kafka.

When the student left, I wondered if my latest vita—sailing under the flag *Facetiae Vincunt Omnia*—would be scuttled by lemon-sucking deans or department heads or if it would surely rise to the top of the pile of competing vitas.

For days, I wondered and waited, waited.

I often silenced the whines of waiting by playing racquet ball with a witty colleague who held a graduate degree from Harvard and who doubled as a part-time farmer. If Geneva cuts me, I thought of leaving my colleague a "trunk thought," compliments of Car Couplet, a thought that invites people to reflect on all that civilization owes, not to the automobile (that is obvious and pedestrian), but to a less obvious cog in the culture. I knew that my friend would want others to interact with the couplet's essential significance, for he would be able to isolate all the foods, drinks, jobs, metaphors, and more that the couplet suggests. The couplet would proclaim:

> It's time for our culture to trace in full
> All that it owes to the seed of the bull.

During that first winter in Pennsylvania, I often stood next to my office window and gazed at the snow parachuting past the dark sandstone of that Victorian Gothic structure that we call Old Main. I envisioned all sorts of distinguished college presidents and administrators sitting in their padded swivel chairs, feet on the desk, clipboards on lap, flair pens in hand. I envisioned them sorting their herd of Ph.D.s into two columns. At the top of one column, I envisioned a label that read: "Sacred Cows."

The other label that I envisioned read: "Hamburgers."

That first December in Pennsylvania, I received a Christmas greeting and a long letter from a friend from the Bloomington days. In the letter, she detailed her adventures as a young scholar on the road in Nebraska, Georgia, California, and Minnesota. The letter profiled the four state universities where she had worked, the odd jobs that she had to do, the peculiar situations that had transformed her from a strong idealist to a sheepish scholar, the strange and somewhat absurd compromises that she had to make in order to acquire or renew the nontenure-track teaching positions that were her lot.

In my response, I wrote a long letter detailing my experiences as an intellectual migrant worker. I concluded the letter by noting, "Geneva is a good school, but I have a feeling they're going to let me go. I'll know for sure in March. If they clip me—and with the job market for Ph.D.s in literature being what it is—I just don't know what I'll do. I'm so, so very tired of sailing thosc letters and vitas in quest of teaching positions, but I suppose I'll do it again. I certainly do not want to go out to San Francisco and wait for the earth to do the polka. Or do I?"

Woodhix Press, publisher of *Albino Cockroaches*, gave up on selling the work and forwarded me all the unsold copies. I signed one and sent it to my friend, for she too was a writer of sorts. I also included a tearsheet of that feature article dealing with the quest for the *Albino* title and dedication.

The Minnesota town where my friend was working was especially cold on that winter day in December when I had mailed her my Christmas greetings: a white card with a pen and ink drawing of a tall, emaciated young man squatting at the periphery of a summer wheat field with legs folded like nut crackers. That day the Communists' savage, bloody, and repulsive reign of terror in Afghanistan dominated the news. On the card I wrote two lines that, at once, alluded to the essence of Christmas, the Afghans' noble struggle, and our academic plight as gypsy scholars. The lines:

> May our quest for Peace, Justice, and tenure-track
> Resemble winter's reach for northern places.

My quest—really "long-shot" hope—for tenure continued, and to it I added the quest for a book publisher. "Most professors," I wrote in a diary entry for February 15, "share many acts, the most obvious of which is: moving. Many move from position to position before they settle into these tenured jobs that'll lead them to their senior citizens' discount cards. Many also move their book or article manuscripts from publisher to publisher before they locate homes for them or—more commonly—before they give up on them and begin to sharpen their attacks on the 'publish or perish' demands of academia."

For a good while, I moved an autobiographic book manuscript with typical professorial eagerness and drive. The cockroach chapbook was poetry, but my new book was prose, identity-crisis prose unpublished prose that resembled that of twenty million other writers—a conservative estimate, perhaps. Whatever, I tried the manuscript on the country's leading commercial publishers, and I persisted in my efforts, for I knew that no editor was going to write or call me and say, "On the left side of your desk, the third drawer from the top, near the rear, under three old student files is a manuscript that we would like to consider for publication if you would only be kind enough to forward it to us."

# PART TWO
# THE GYPSY MANUSCRIPT

*CHAPTER FIVE*

# The Commercial Side of Publishers Row

It was easy enough to write about my life as a gypsy scholar teaching English, coaching football, and working at the writer's craft. But to get that life professionally published as a book was another matter. I wrote it up into a seventy-thousand-word book manuscript and began the long and agonizing search for a publisher. Along the way, I learned much about the publishing world of New York and other places. I, in effect, learned more about the writer's craft.

I entitled the manuscript *The Gypsy Scholar*, a title that alluded to Matthew Arnold's famous poem "The Scholar-Gypsy." I wrote an extensive prospectus on the manuscript, consisting of a summary of the narrative, a brief assessment of its audience and how to reach it, a chapter by chapter review of its contents, and a reference to the excerpt from the manuscript that had appeared in the *Chronicle of Higher Education*. Then I went to the library, isolated several publishers who specialized in publishing books on higher education, examined their catalogues, and ranked them in order of my preference. I mailed the prospectus to what I felt was the best, if not the biggest, publisher in the higher education field. In the *Literary Market Place*, a book that lists all publishers and their personnel, I noticed the name of the president of the company; none of the editors was listed, so I wrote directly to the president. A week later, the president's response arrived, and from it—as indeed from all the other letters that are here reproduced verbatim, though the names and dates are omitted—I learned useful lessons. The entire letter stated:

Dear Mr. Hanna,

Thank you for writing to me about your plans for a book on "The Gypsy Scholar." I had earlier read and enjoyed your essay in the *Chronicle*. The chapter descriptions are both amusing and sad.

We could not successfully publish your book. We could not sell it. There was a time when I might have been able to publish such light-hearted books about the plights of young academics, but those days are long past. The only people who read my books are college administrators. Faculty do not read outside their increasingly narrow specialties. (I just heard but choose not to believe that Berkeley just hired an early Milton specialist, whatever that might be. Poor guy must not know he is suspended between paradises.)

Your conjecture about the audience and marketing is about as realistic as your receiving an offer as a tenured full professor of English at Harvard in tomorrow's mail.

This book idea of yours just might find a publisher rewritten as a novel. Trade books with educational settings are usually disasters, but you should try. I doubt a press with an academic agenda could do the book justice. I could not.

I would have liked to write more encouragingly. I appreciate your courtesy in writing to me.

Very truly yours,

[Signed]

President of the Company

That letter was neatly typed and signed in the president's absence by his secretary. Ten days later, a handwritten note arrived from the same president. The note stated:

> Hello Mr. Hanna,
>
> I have no fountain pen at hand, and refuse to write with a ball point.
>
> I had not told you I had sent your letter and enclosures to my old friend _____ _____, figuring she would see no potential. I am pleased that she, too, found your idea provocative. Ms. _____ is an exceptionally able and perceptive editor. Please be very careful about what you send to her. Please do not send inadequate materials that are not fully revealing of your talent and, more importantly, your story. Ms. _____ is a good developmental editor (meaning how to help an author develop the best potential from a *promising* ms.), but she will not tell you how to write the book. That is your job. Let me know results.
>
> Ms. _____ is one of the best editors at one of the best trade publishers. I am pleased for you that she has taken a personal interest in your book. Work hard to please her—and best wishes.
>
> > Yours cordially,
> >
> > [Signed]
> >
> > President of the Company
>
> N.B.:
> (*No* carbons to anyone)

The president's letter and his follow-up note indicated to me the warmth and concern that the gentleman publisher-editor often expresses, the same kind of concern that informs the correspondence of, say, Maxwell E. Perkins of Scribner's. A day after the follow-up note arrived, a letter from an executive editor at one of America's leading trade publishers appeared in my mailbox. The letter stated:

> Dear Mr. Hanna:
>
> An old publishing colleague, _____ _____, has sent me your proposal and outline. If you have a couple of

chapters of *The Gypsy Scholar* in manuscript form, I'd be interested in seeing them.

Sincerely,

[Signed]

Executive Editor

Immediately, I sent the manuscript's prologue and opening chapter. Three weeks later, they came back with this letter:

Dear Mr. Hanna:

Thank you very much for the chance to see the prologue and opening chapter of *The Gypsy Scholar.* I enjoyed reading it—although it's hard to use the word "enjoy" in connection with a subject that is so personally disappointing to many more-than-qualified people and that is such a black mark on the educational situation in the country.

As a book-length publishing project, *The Gypsy Scholar* poses certain difficulties. To me it has to be either a black comic novel or a more detached report. Now I think it's too personal and would appeal mainly to people in a similar situation, most of whom probably aren't buying books these days.

If you rework the material in any substantial way or develop any other book projects, please let me know.

With my best regards,

Sincerely,

[Signed]

Executive Editor

It took me three weeks to rework the nonfiction book manuscript into a novel; I reasoned that since a major commercial house was interested in seeing the work, I wanted to act while the interest was hot and before the editor leaps to another house. The response to the entire novel came back quickly. It stated:

Dear Mr. Hanna:

Thank you for sending the manuscript for *The Gypsy Scholar*. Seldom has someone been able to act on an editorial suggestion so quickly.

The novel is smooth and well written, and there are many strikingly funny scenes. It seems to me, though, that the device of telling flattens the narrative. For the general reader and general publisher, this would pose some problems. Let me try another suggestion: submit the manuscript to one of the small companies that are publishing new writers and new writing. I think you may find an audience there.

Again, all good luck.

Sincerely,

[Signed]

Executive Editor

That was round one, as it were. At the end of it, I had, not one published book, but two unpublished ones—though both used the same materials. To be sure, in fictionalizing *The Gypsy Scholar*, I injected it with tension built around a student-professor love affair. I wrote a query letter dealing with the novel, and I sent the letter to fifteen major New York publishers. The letter stated:

Dear Editor:

*Oklahoma Wins an Oscar* takes place at Kickapoo College, a state school in Oklahoma. There, Paul P. Prisca, a latter-day Ph.D., teaches Aquinas, Dante, and Goethe to Sooners, Indians, jocks, rodeo queens, literary buffs, drug culture leftovers, and other minds strapped in America's cowboy ghetto.

Paul differs from the conventional literature professor. At times, for example, he doubles as an assistant football coach for the Bears of Kickapoo. At other times, he lectures by reading to his classes samples from his Kafkaesque prose fiction.

Throughout his stay in Kickapoo, Paul flushes out his

students' sense of humor, which he finds to be surprisingly funny. His life complicates itself when he falls in love with a student, an act that leads the student to confide in the shrink at the college, and the shrink, in turn, confides in the administration. Both acts lead Paul to perplexing, indeed tragic, pursuits.

*Oklahoma Wins an Oscar* offers a slice of life from America's Southwest; it explores the dimensions of a regional culture, and it does it in a refreshingly positive and informative way; and it footnotes the absurd compromises that many Ph.D.s are making during the job squeeze of the last quarter of the twentieth century.

The potential is there for a movie tie-in, for the novel has various levels of tension, a professor-student love affair, a number of engaging characters, and a fresh portrayal of a facet of American life. The novel's humor—realized through one-liners, through peculiar and ironic subplots, and through Paul's picaresque ways—will make for an entertaining movie. The unusual circumstances leading to Paul's death give the novel a poignancy that might well interest a movie maker.

*Oklahoma Wins an Oscar* is typed and available for immediate rejection. Might you be interested in considering this 65,000 word narrative for publication? If so, I shall be pleased to forward it to you at once. If you prefer, I shall forward its opening chapters.

I look forward to hearing from you.

Sincerely,

S. S. HANNA

English Department

Six publishers invited me to submit the novel, and all rejected it. Some letters were brief and to the point, leading me to speculate whether the reader reached page seven. Here's a sample:

Dear. S. S. Hanna:
Thanks for sending me *Oklahoma Wins an Oscar*. I found your novel to be different and interesting, but I don't

think it has a wide enough appeal for us to feel we could do well with it.

Best of luck placing your manuscript elsewhere.

Sincerely,

[Signed]

Editor

Other letters, however, indicated to me that the entire novel was read with care. Here is a sample from a large and prestigious New York house.

Dear Professor Hanna:

I must begin by apologizing for the tardiness of this response to your novel, *Oklahoma Wins an Oscar*. The press of the holiday season, when colleagues are away and we have less frequent editorial board meetings, has caused this delay in our coming to a decision on your manuscript. We have now reached that decision and I am sorry to report that we must decline to make an offer of publication for the novel.

Those of us who read the novel found much in it to admire. The portrait of Kickapoo College and the send-up of the vagaries and banalities of academic politics are indeed funny. But I also feel there are problems, chief among them the character of Paul, who, it seems to me, wanders through the novel like a cipher. Now perhaps that is your intention—to present Paul as a sort of intellectual and emotional lump of clay who allowed himself (with one exception) to be molded by the circumstances of academic life, especially life at Kickapoo. The trouble is, such a cipher, even in a comic novel, is hard for the reader to identify with. Paul and his predicament elicited in me no strong feeling beyond puzzled bemusement. In the end, despite his adventure as a football coach, his affair with Sonia, and so on, Paul's story does not sufficiently engage the reader—or this reader anyway.

I do thank you for allowing me to consider *Oklahoma Wins an Oscar.*

> Yours sincerely,
>
> [Signed]
>
> Editor

One week in late January, I received two rejection letters: Monday, *The Gypsy Scholar* came back; Thursday, *Oklahoma Wins an Oscar* showed up. Friday, I placed both manuscripts on my office desk and had a little talk with them, as it were. I wondered what to do with them. I finally decided to put the novel on the "back burner" and concentrate on marketing *The Gypsy Scholar.* I still wanted to try the first-rate commercial houses, but now I moved my focus away from New York and set it on Boston. I wrote a major publisher in Boston a query letter on *The Gypsy Scholar,* and I received this reply:

Dear Mr. Hanna:
  I would be interested in seeing the manuscript of *The Gypsy Scholar* if you would like to send it along. I would say it's a long shot, but then you probably realize that everything is a long shot.

  Best wishes,

  [Signed]

  Editor

Of course, I instantly forwarded the entire manuscript. With it I enclosed a simple cover letter, thanking the editor for inviting me to submit the work and hoping that it would not "disappoint" him. I eagerly awaited the editor's reply, which came in less than a month. It stated:

Dear Mr. Hanna:
  Thank you for sending *The Gypsy Scholar.* In your covering letter, you said that you hoped it wouldn't disappoint me. It didn't disappoint me at all, but unfortu-

nately it is still not a book we can publish. I would like to emphasize that I am speaking only for one particular publisher, and the decision has more to do with our needs and goals than with the quality of the manuscript. I won't go into too much detail about why we can't publish the book, because I suspect it might be ideal for another publisher. The crux of the matter is that we try to publish books for the general reader or for a few specialized audiences we know well. This book seems directed at a couple of specialized audiences we don't know well. The first part of the book seems aimed at gypsy scholars themselves (alas, perhaps not a very good audience for a commercial publisher, since many have to watch their book budgets carefully), the second part more at evangelical Christians. I don't know what publisher would be well suited to reach the first audience, but I presume a religious publisher would know the second audience.

What you might have here is the makings of two books for two different groups. I wish you the best of luck in finding a publisher for one or both of them.

I should mention that this is one of the few manuscripts I have read completely through even though I could see it didn't fall within our areas of interest. Once I got started, I couldn't put it down. You may wonder, then, whether that isn't more important than the book fitting in the right categories. Realistically it's not, because an editor is only one link in the publishing chain and has to be pragmatic about whether the other links can support the book.

Best wishes,

[Signed]

Editor, Trade Division


I took half of the Boston editor's implied advice and forwarded *The Gypsy Scholar* to a well-known evangelical house where an editor-friend of mine labored. He rejected the manuscript but recommended that I try a university press with it. His entire letter said:

Dear S.S.:

I am beside myself (which is difficult without astral projection). I kid you not—I was thinking about you three days before your query about *The Gypsy Scholar* arrived. You rascal. No wonder you're a gypsy—after what you did to ex-cronie! Joshing, I assure you.

Maybe you're like me. You haven't decided exactly who you are—a Christian, yes, but what does God have for you? You're a professor at Geneva College. I'm a book editor here at _____ and (as it is today) I want to retire here. BUT there are so many creative and intellectual channels in which I wish to swim. Sad to admit it, too, I'm not a dreamer. I'm not a gypsy.

Consider the richness of your life up until now—the weird experiences, the travel (although perhaps not always voluntary), the exposure to the wide spectrum of life (bully, what a phrase!). Believe it or not, your career and life will jell (or is it gel?). You have to recognize it, too. You're a Cassandra and a Gadfly, and I use those in an admirable sense. I want to be the fly, but I'm merely part of the ointment.

What can I say that I haven't already? We can't publish *The Gypsy Scholar*, but you might write to Dr. _____ _____ at _____ University Press. They are doing a number of avant garde books. I still like that phrase.

I wish to heaven you could engage a good literary agent in New York. Honest, though, I don't know a good literary agent! I have read every word of your *Gypsy*, including my close friend, Dr. _____ _____, who is a philosophy graduate from Vanderbilt. He is editor of general religious books here (Chief Editor, no less). He's also a frustrated professor! He is also wild about your writing and the possibilities.

With a heavy heart I return your sample materials via book rate. Write me about your idea. Please. I am dreadfully (love that Sir Cedric word) sorry that we can't click on this one.

Fraternally yours,

[Signed, first name only]

Editor

Should I try the university press that the evangelical editor had recommended? How about other university presses? Might they consider a liberated manuscript, one that is free from footnotes? I asked myself these and other questions. At one instance, I remembered two former colleagues and dear friends of mine at Oklahoma, and I especially recalled their experiences with a certain university press in the Southwest. Both had sent the press their doctoral dissertations. One was accepted and published, and in five years it earned the author $123.29. The other doctoral dissertation was rejected and returned, but it was returned damaged due to a fire at the press. Thanks to an insurance claim, the press enclosed a $300.00 check with the partly barbecued manuscript.

My friends' experiences were at the forefront of my mind when I invited the editors and directors of the country's university presses to discover me. The university press folks responded variously. In some cases, they surprised and shocked me.

## CHAPTER SIX

# University Presses and Literary Agents

Geneva College's *Literary Market Place* helped me greatly in my search for a publisher for *The Gypsy Scholar;* it supplied me with the names, addresses, and phone numbers of all the directors and editors at the country's university presses. I addressed the directors or editors by name and sent them a detailed prospectus on *The Gypsy Scholar*— listing a summary of the work, its audience, sales potential, and chapter contents—and the following cover letter:

Dear Editor:

Might you be interested in considering for publication my recently completed nonfiction book manuscript? It deals with a seldom studied facet of contemporary higher education in America: the gypsy scholars. Enclosed is the book's prospectus. Should you wish to read the entire manuscript, I shall be pleased to forward it to you at once.

Sincerely,

S. S. HANNA

English Department

Enclosure
SSH/TRS-80

The responses of the university press folks fell into several categories. One category consisted of brief and formal letters declining the opportunity to read the manuscript. They are not the kind of letters one takes home to show his or her spouse. Here is a sample from a word processor at a large Eastern press:

Dear Professor Hanna:
Thank you for your recent letter describing your manuscript. We have carefully considered your proposal, but regretfully I must report that we have determined that your project would not be well suited to our present publishing program.
We thank you for thinking of our press and wish you success with your work.

Sincerely,

[Signed]

Humanities Editor

A second category of responses must have been written by editors who in real life would probably couch a negative reply by using the phrase "not really." Here is a sample:

Dear Dr. Hanna:
Thank you for your letter of the 24th and for considering our press for the publication of your manuscript *The Gypsy Scholar.*
Your proposal sounds like a marvelous idea and would certainly meet a need in the publishing market. I read your synopsis with real pleasure, but, alas, your work is not for us. We are not adverse to trying to reach a general interest audience, but our primary target is the scholarly community. Consequently, our publishing interests lie in the area of making available to that august group the fruits of some scholar's activities.
What have you done with your dissertation? Has it been published? If not and if you feel it might be worthy of

publication, perhaps we may yet still have need of more correspondence.

Sincerely,

[Signed]

Director

A third category of responses, written by editors who gave the manuscript the baseball equivalent of a base on balls only to strike out the side, suggested that the book was not for them, though a different treatment might well be. Here is a sample from a large press in the West:

Dear Dr. Hanna:

Sorry but THE GYPSY SCHOLAR doesn't sound like a university press book—though I'd think a commercial press might like it. I've often thought that a sociological book on THE INTELLECTUAL AS MIGRANT LABOR would be a nice project, but it would have to be done in a "properly" impersonal way.

Sincerely,

[Signed]

Editor

A fourth category stuttered through a "Yes, we'd read this, but . . ." type letter. Here is a sample:

Dear Dr. Hanna:

Your book is not quite our usual fare, but let us have a look. I'd like it in hand by April 25th so I can present it to the editorial committee for at least a preliminary response. (The discussion will be spirited.) If it's really not for us, I'll know quickly and can return it quickly. If we undertake a review, we'll take the usual several weeks.

I will have to ask your assurance that we will be the only press reviewing the work at this time.

Sincerely,

[Signed]

Editorial Committee Chairman

A fifth category of responses gave an enthusiastic "Yes, we'd read it." They formed the "show-and-tell-your-spouse" type letters. Here is a sample:

Dear Professor Hanna:

I would be very glad to have the opportunity to read your manuscript *The Gypsy Scholar* and would like to invite you to send it on at your earliest convenience. I suspect we might be a little more receptive to a book of this kind than most university presses—we aren't afraid of nontraditional books and have a fairly substantial list of publications on higher education.

Your prospectus is an impressive one—and demonstrates that you can put words together in a way that is at least acceptable and might be considerably better than that.

Yours Sincerely

[Signed]

Director and Editor

A sixth category consisted of negative replies, spliced by quick lectures on the scope and purposes of scholarly publishing. Most of the editors in this group had read the prospectus *and* the opening parts of the manuscript. Here is a sample from a Big Ten university press:

Dear Mr. Hanna:

Thank you for sending the prospectus and opening parts of *The Gypsy Scholar*. I read it from beginning to end and was fascinated by it. I look forward to being able to read the entire work in published form.

And now, the bad news. It is not really for us. It is the purpose of a university press, as you certainly are aware, to disseminate the results of scholarly research. Any manuscript that does not meet this criterion must demonstrate some other special quality that the publisher is seeking for his list. In our case, we do publish some titles of regional interest that are not always purely works of scholarship but are of value to the general reader in this area.

I cannot suggest any particular publisher to you, although I would think that university presses would not be the most appropriate for your manuscript. The best course, probably, is to go first to those who have published books most similar to yours. You might also consider contacting a literary agent.

Again, thank you for considering us for what is obviously an interesting and instructive manuscript. Please let me know when you find a publisher.

Sincerely,

[Signed]

Assistant Director


P.S. The book prospectus and other materials are enclosed.


A seventh category consisted of editors or directors who were negative but helpful. What they said amounted to this: "Don't write us, write others." They suggested the names of publishers to approach, and like editors from other groups, they promised to buy copies of *The Gypsy Scholar* when another house publishes it. The sample in this category comes from a large and leading Ivy League university press:


Dear Professor Hanna:

I enjoyed reading your prospectus for "The Gypsy Scholar."

I would love to read the manuscript, but I have to be honest and tell you that I think there is no more chance of publishing it here than flying to the moon. It would be fun to publish, but an editor's prerogative in a scholarly house does not extend so far as justifying publication of a book to satisfy his whims. There is a serious message in your book, of course, and no doubt many people in the academic world could learn much from it. However, if we were to publish it, the work would have to be transformed from a personal essay into a stodgy, jargon-filled, footnote-crammed sociological tract, and I wouldn't wish that fate upon you, given all that you have already suffered from the Furies of Academe.

My suggestion is that you try to find an enterprising publisher among one of the smaller commercial houses, perhaps _____ or _____, for I think it is that kind of house which would be able to do justice to this rather unusual kind of book. Maybe even _____ _____ who likes unusual projects, would be interested. Or you might try _____ _____. If you have not already done so, I would also urge you to get in touch with _____ _____, the director of the _____ University Press; that press has published a lot in folklore and maybe your manuscript will be viewed as a contribution to that field, among others.

Whatever happens, I will look forward to your book's publication and will be among the first to buy a copy. Please let me know which house will be doing it.

Yours cheerfully,

[Signed]

Assistant Director

An eighth category also consisted of editors who had read the prospectus and the early parts of the manuscript. Their responses tried to resonate with the humor of the prose that I had enclosed. Here is a sample from a Southern press written by an editor who must rank as the country's number two word jock; the number one, of course, is Howard Cosell. The complete letter stated:

Dear S. S.:

I returned to my desk (following a two-weeks stint in Baltimore of all places) to find your letter (with enclosures) about two-thirds the way into the pile. I am answering your query at my earliest.

It is interesting—*The Gypsy Scholar*, that is. It is not within the purview (as we editors-in-chief say) of our present publishing program. Yet is still is interesting, and we do occasionally break through the restraints imposed upon us (by ourselves) by our "purview parameters." (We must, of course, limit ourselves to those areas wherein we possess at least some modicum of expertise: we would not, for example, even consider a manuscript on the Vietnam fiasco since no one has any expertise whatsoever in that area.)

So I am not opening the file on your offering. Rather I am referring your offering into the capable hands of our very best acquisition editor. Aformentioned editor himself is in possession of a bona fide Ph.D. (at last mention unrecalled), and, although he is well esconced in academe, he will appreciate your subject because he is still something of a gypsy at heart.

I am sure our acquisitions editor will have something to say, and I will forthwith inform you concerning his recommendation and any reaction to that recommendation.

In the meantime please do not open any other files until you hear from me—and you will.

You are welcome,

[Signed]

Editor-in-Chief

One day, I decided to go beyond forwarding the prospectus and/or sample chapters; I pulled out the name of an MIT editor from the *Literary Market Place* and forwarded the editor the *entire* manuscript. Two months later, the manuscript came back, rejected with enthusiasm. It carried not one but two rejection letters. One letter was long and helpful; the second was "one-of-a-kind." First the long one:

Dear Professor Hanna:
   I don't know where you got my name or what made you submit your manuscript to the MIT Press, but I'm glad you did.

I know there's a readership for this book; I think there's a publisher for it. If there's not, you'll have gathered enough anecdotal material and documentary evidence along the way to write a satire of the publishing industry.

But I knew shortly after I began reading that this was not for us; what little autobiographical material we publish is by scientists—typically a former child-prodigy now in his dotage, and spending summers on Martha's Vineyard decides it's time to fill the world in about his contribution to the discovery of penicillin, the development of nuclear fission, the advances in theoretical physics, etc. Invariably one of Herr Dr. Emeritus's former students, fondly remembered in the memoir as "an exceptionally gifted undergraduate" and now a professor at MIT, sits on our Editorial Board. . . . You fill in the rest.

Anyway, I like your story and the way it's told, as did three of my colleagues here at the Press with whom I shared the manuscript for the fun of it. We're all defectors from academia, and probably feel some guilt for getting out and consequently have an interest in reading the first-hand reports of POWs like yourself who are still being moved from camp to camp.

I'm going to make a couple of suggestions. I think you should be approaching trade houses, not university presses. This isn't a scholarly book; it's a very engaging and wry piece of nonfiction for an academic audience. Who publishes this kind of thing? If I were you I would try some of the smaller and more literary trade houses. The _____ _____ would seem to be a good bet. Write to _____ _____, the new Director. They are known for their flair.

Another good independent press is _____ _____. Write to _____ _____, Editorial Director. With her, you can use my name, and I think you'll get a serious reading. On the West Coast, try _____ _____. The editor there is _____ _____. These are all good but small trade houses.

If you want a trade editor's attention from any of the big New York houses, you should get an agent. I think you've got a property you can eventually sell, but I think an agent could place it much more quickly. I'll give you a name of someone I know who is young and open to new writers, and who happens to work for one of the classier

New York agencies. _____ _____ is with [Name and Address of the Agency]. He's still building a list of writers, not yet having lunch at the Four Seasons with Mario Puzo and Gore Vidal. You can tell him that I suggested you write to him. All these people can still laugh. Trusting you can still take a joke too, I improvised the enclosed rejection letter for you, inspired by your *Chronicle* stunt mentioned in the manuscript. I wish you luck with this, and hope you'll let me know what happens.

S. S. Hanna has a minicult of followers among the MIT editors; I realize that won't get you anywhere on the subway, but we thank you for writing this.

Sincerely,

[Signed]

Editor

The "one-of-a-kind" rejection note was typed on a separate sheet; it consisted of four lines that generated in me a strong laugh. The note said:

> We regret that this is not the
> shit we are currently eating.
> Thank you for giving us the
> opportunity to consider it.
>
> THE EDITORS

I tested the wisdom of the generous and kind MIT editor by forwarding a copy of *The Gypsy Scholar* to the New York literary agent that he had recommended. The agent's reply stated:

Dear Mr. Hanna:

Thanks very much for giving us a chance with *The Gypsy Scholar*. Clearly you can write and I too found the manuscript fun to read. However, despite the smooth style and excellent writing here, I feel your subject limits the promise of a wide enough audience necessary to attract a commercial publisher, and I am therefore, returning the work.

If you should decide to fictionalize this account or are in the midst of a new work, I'd love to take a look. I'm impressed with your obvious talent and am sorry not to have the right enthusiasm for *Gypsy Scholar*.

The best of luck to you and your work and I hope to hear from you in the future.

Yours,

[Signed]

The Literary Agent

One day, I read an engaging article in *Scholarly Publishing*, the professional journal of the university presses, written by an imaginative director at a major press. So, I sent the director-author the first two chapters of *The Gypsy Scholar*. He wrote back and asked for the rest. I sent the entire manuscript at once. He opened it, read it, liked it, rejected it for his press, but took the liberty to forward it to a friend of his, a highly respected New York literary agent. The agent enjoyed the entire manuscript and agreed to add it to the list that she offered to the trade.

Such a positive development pleased me, but it failed to change my life. I continued to pay the rent and buy the groceries out of my college salary, and I was wise to do so, for the rejection letters kept coming to my house, though now they started to make a slight detour via my agent's office in New York. The agent's submissions were made to the first-rate publishers and, for the most part, to senior editors. The agent tended to receive quicker readings on the manuscript than I had received, and her rejection letters tended to be shorter than mine. Here are three letters grouped according to "height":

Dear [Agent's first name]
Thanks for sending *The Gypsy Scholar* by S. S. Hanna.

It's not right for our list but I'd be interested in seeing anything else Mr. Hanna plans to write.

Cordially,

[Signed, first name]

Senior Editor

Dear [Agent's first name]

Thanks for sending S. S. Hanna's *The Gypsy Scholar* to me. I've read it while laughing, which is far more than I can say for most of the humorous manuscripts I've read this month. Alas, although I did laugh I can't quite see the market for the book. So it's back to you with my sincere thanks.

Best,

[Signed, first name]

Senior Editor

Dear [Agent's first name]

It was mighty kind of you to send Dr. Hanna's manuscript to me. For personal reasons I found it particularly interesting. Over the years my father taught in a dozen major universities and one of my daughters is married to a Ph.D. who has been kicked around considerably.

I think it is an excellent book, but I do not believe we could present it successfully. The manuscript is going back to you herewith. I hope you have good luck with it.

Best wishes,

[Signed, first name]

Senior Editor

With the agent pursuing the commercial houses, I concentrated on trying more directors at university presses. I liked the long MIT rejection letter so much that I enclosed it with a submission of the entire manuscript to a director at one of America's most prestigious university presses. The humanities editor at this press had earlier rejected the manuscript via a freshly typed form letter. I felt that the enclosed rejection letter might arouse the director's interest, and it might also serve as a screening report on the manuscript. Three weeks later, the manuscript came back with a frank and illuminating letter:

Dear Dr. Hanna:

Like my colleagues at MIT, I enjoyed your manuscript; and like them, I cannot accept it for publication. I asked our editorial director to read it, too, knowing he would enjoy it as much as I did. He did. Enjoy it, that is. And concurred in my judgement that even if we pushed hard for publication our faculty editorial board would not confer the blessing without which we may not publish any book.

You *might* find a university press able to take on your book, but I am dubious. If you want to go that route still, _____ University Press is probably your best bet. The director of that press is appropriately irreverent and seems not to owe his faculty board—which some say does not exist—as much obeisance as is required of the rest of us. You may tell him I told you this if you wish.

I hope you get the book published, but I think you'll get better odds on the commerical side of Publishers Row.

Sincerely,

[Signed]

The Director

That director did not know that I had tried—and, indeed, now had an agent who was trying—my odds on the commercial side of Publishers Row. Still, I refused to give up on either Row, for I, too, had a dream, a dream that someone somewhere will one day want to publish *The Gypsy Scholar.* One night I dreamt that a major New York publisher accepted the manuscript, but several months later the publisher hit hard times and returned all accepted manuscripts—including *The Gypsy Scholar*—to their authors. Before emerging from the dream, I found myself saying,

"*Gypsy* has ten chapters, but why is the publisher filing papers for Chapter Eleven?"

That dream, oddly enough, could be traced to actual life experiences. At one point in my writing career, the prestigious *Texas Quarterly* of the University of Texas in Austin accepted a long article of mine; an editor copyedited the manuscript, asked me to approve the edited version, had the manuscript type set, and scheduled it for publication in a future issue. I added the article to the publication list on my vita. One day, I received a large yellow envelope from the *Texas Quarterly;* I expected it to contain reprints of the published article; it contained, instead, the copyedited manuscript, the proofs, and a typed letter that explained the circumstances leading to the *Quarterly's* death.

On another occasion, I submitted three identical poems to the *Mediterranean Review* and to another literary forum; the editors of both forums wrote me pleasant acceptance letters. The *Mediterranean Review*, however, requested a picture of me to run with the poems. Since I could not legally publish the poems in both places, I recalled them from the "other" forum and, in the process, angered its editor. Then I went out and paid a professional photographer for an artistic shot of my face; I mailed the photograph to the review. A year or so later, I received a little package containing the unpublished poems, the picture, and this handwritten but unsigned note, "Sorry, *MR* is no longer being published. Defunct, to be exact."

"You don't publish deathless prose and poems in defunct magazines," I told myself as I popped the poems and the picture into a desk drawer and forgot about them. I was unable to forget about *The Gypsy Scholar*. I tinkered with it: I replaced the title with a flashier one; I toned down the new title by a staid subtitle; I tried writing a brand new preface, then I rewrote the old one; and finally, I packaged the entire manuscript with the standard *Gypsy Scholar* title (and the old-new preface) and mailed it to a prolific writer, a nationally recognized thinker from the University of Chicago. Having read some of his writings, I knew that the topic would interest him; and if it interested him enough to want to see the manuscript in print, I asked him to kindly consider forwarding it to an editor of his choice. As it turned out, the manuscript pleased him, and he sent it—with a strong cover letter—to an editor-friend of his who worked at one of America's oldest and best known commercial houses. The Chicago thinker concluded his letter by noting, "Here is a talent that should not be denied."

Well, the editor took the "not" out, and presto—I was denied. But I refused to give up on *The Gypsy Scholar.* I continued my struggles to place it with a university or a commercial publisher, and my struggles took a potentially promising turn.

## CHAPTER SEVEN

# Publishers Weekly
## *and Literary Suicide*

A number of the letters that I had received from the editors
and directors at the university presses were published as
part of an article in *Publishers Weekly: The Journal of the
Book Industry.* In the article I celebrated—albeit with an
ironic touch—my failure to locate a publisher for *The Gypsy
Scholar.* Xeroxing and mailing the book manuscript had cost
a little less than $300.00. *Publishers Weekly* paid me $390.00
for my rejection letters. When the check arrived, I began to
feel that there may yet be some justice in the literary world,
for the lead article in that influencial magazine brought me
a nice check—and more.

Several editors from major commercial houses in New
York wrote and called asking to see the entire manuscript
of *The Gypsy Scholar.* I sent it with high hopes to one publisher at a time. Here is the written response of a senior
editor who had called:

Dear. S. S. Hanna:
I'm returning herewith *The Gypsy Scholar.* I found the
book amusing, and there is certainly evidence of the wit,

humor, and irony that I saw in the Publisher's Weekly piece. However, this is simply too specialized a subject for me to take the book on at _____. There's an audience for the book—but not a wide enough one for it to make sense for us. I'm sorry I can't be more helpful. I'd suggest you continue to approach some of the more adventurous university presses and some of the regional presses.

Thanks for letting me take a look at this project. Good luck with it.

Regards,

[Signed]

Senior Editor

That response resembled a second one from another senior editor at a major New York publisher. The second response stated:

Dear Mr. Hanna:

Thank you for sending your manuscript for *The Gypsy Scholar* to me for my consideration.

I am surprised that you did not have success with university presses; the book strikes me as a work that would fit in nicely with their lists. In any case, I am afraid that *The Gypsy Scholar* is not an _____ tradebook. I suggest that you try other houses, however. Happily, the American publishing industry has ranging tastes and is not easily defined.

I wish you good fortune in your quest, and remain

Yours sincerely,

[Signed]

Senior Editor

A third response consisted of an even kinder "no." It came from the manager of special markets at a huge New York press. The letter stated:

Dear Mr. Hanna:

First of all, please forgive the delay in my getting back to you; I have been out of town for a month and have only just returned. I must say that I enjoyed reading *The Gypsy Scholar* and it is with very mixed feelings that I find myself following suit with the subjects of your *PW* article and in fact, sending what amounts to yet another rejection letter.

*The Gypsy Scholar* does work for me, and it did provide me with "some fun reading—and more." But right now we are looking for more universal themes for our _____ books, and as interesting as your experience is, it does not offer the breadth of shared experience that we're striving for in our books right now.

Thank you again. You're probably tired of hearing this, but I do wish you luck in securing another publisher. Please feel free to be in touch if you have any other ideas that you'd like to pursue; you're obviously an extremely talented writer.

Sincerely,

[Signed]

Manager, Special Markets

As a change of pace, I thought I might go back and try the university presses again, but this time instead of trying editors, I would try directors, and instead of forwarding a conventional cover letter, I would forward an unconventional one. I had read a book on university presses, and I was a regular reader of their forum *Scholarly Publishing*; I knew that even if an editor liked a manuscript and wanted to secure evaluations for it from outside readers, the editor still needed the approval of the director. So in writing the director (usually a former editor), I was, in effect, bypassing the middle person. The unconventional letter stated:

Dear Director:

The enclosed nonfiction book manuscript might stimulate a variety of responses from you. Sketched below are likely possibilities. There are others. Please consider circling one or more of the suggested responses; if need be, please devise your own.

A. This work is just . . . too much. You've got to continue to correspond with yourself, kid. Here is your Self-Addressed Stamped Envelope and manuscript. Good luck.

B. I liked the portrait of the Seminole Indian lady (pp. 61–62 and 74–75) who sold you her hair-growing herbs. Perhaps she has a formula to get this thing published. Or maybe that aging con woman Gladys Princeton (pp. 175–76) could concoct the magic formula.

C. Burn this nonsense.

D. The "trunk thoughts" delineated in the Geneva chapter (pp. 178–79 and 189–90) intrigued us. Could you design one for university press people?

E. If I gave you a nickel for every laugh that the script had generated, you'd be able to buy lots of bazooka bubble gums. Unfortunately, however, our faculty advisory board members do not laugh or chew or go with girls who do.

F. Enclosed is a nasty/nice letter, but don't you dare use it in any future piece for *Publishers Weekly.*

G. Now that the AAUP has a Golden Fluke Award, we might just snatch it with the manuscript you had enclosed. It arrived safely, and we plan to give it a serious reading.

H. *The Gypsy Scholar* makes as much sense for our list as does the slogan "The Nation's Geriatrics Ward" make for the license plates of Florida. Sorry.

I. I've read stupid stuff, I've read superstupid stuff, but this is superduper stupid stuff. Follow option "C" and shove it—in the fireplace.

Sincerely,

S. S. HANNA

English Department

The unconventional cover letter and *The Gypsy Scholar*

brought this conventional response from the press of a major state university in the East:

> Dear S. S. Hanna:
>     I have enjoyed reading your manuscript; it is funny, engaging, intelligent, and serious in its own way. I am surprised, really, that after all your efforts to find a publisher (and particularly after your amusing article in *Publishers Weekly* last November) you still don't have a contract.
>     It seems to me that it would be a mistake to publish the book in novelized form and an awful blunder to try to transform it into a formal sociological study. What you need is not a new approach, but a new set of publishers to approach. Why do you persist in sending the manuscript to university presses? Why not send it to _____ _____, say, or one of the more enlightened trade publishers? Perhaps you have done this already, and you surely must have enough earnest advice from university press editors.
>     So, no, I am sorry to say we are not prepared to take on *The Gypsy Scholar*. Chances are we would be criticized for publishing the book and you would be disappointed in our performance. I do wish you good luck with it.
>
> Cordially,
>
> [Signed]
>
> Director
>
> P.S. If you are ever in this area, please give me a call. I'd enjoy meeting you.

I tried another unconventional cover letter on a senior editor at a large university press in the West. The letter read:

> Dear Editor:
>     Here's what you're about to do—and I dread it. You are going to read the title and the first few pages, answer

an interrupting phone call, read the next page, scratch your head, then reach for the enclosed self-addressed stamped envelope, tuck *The Gypsy Scholar* back in, and exclaim: "This fellow has got to correspond with himself; this is just too much."

Of course I would be delighted if you prove me wrong, i.e., if you read on and on. I would be overjoyed if you consider the enclosed as a possible addition to your list. I could tell you of the obscure academic quarterlies and the few well-known places where I had published. But why bother? If the enclosed can't hold your interest, all the other publications are of no value.

If the enclosed works, it should be fun reading—and more. Thank you for considering it.

Sincerely,

S. S. HANNA

English Department

The response to that letter and the manuscript was also negative, but it saved me a little money. It stated:

Dear Professor Hanna,

Ms. _____ is away on a working vacation in England and I am handling her correspondence in her absence. Your manuscript did not receive quite the reading you expected: there were no interrupting phone calls, no interrupting meetings. We are loath to tuck the manuscript back into the self-addressed envelope you sent, so we are sending it back postage paid by us. The work is humorous and I can sympathize with your experiences, but you already anticipated our decision. The work simply doesn't fit our list. Have you tried a trade house? (A question you must have already heard.) It seems clear that there is a best-selling novel here somewhere.

Sincerely,

[Signed]

Editorial Assistant

The only thing that seemed clear to me was that publishers of all sorts were staying clear of *The Gypsy Scholar*. One day I received a telephone call from a professor at the College of Medicine at the University of Oklahoma. He was so intrigued by the article in *Publishers Weekly* that he wondered whether I would consider sending him the entire manuscript "not to publish, but to read," as he repeated several times. I had an extra xerox copy around the office, so I sent it. A week later I received this letter:

Dear Dr. Hanna:

　　I received your manuscript the other day and could hardly put it down. I read the whole thing clear through the first day. It is extremely well written and a very thoughtful, provocative, as well as humorous piece. I would very much like to see it in print. I have been involved with a number of schools that you mention in the manuscript and, therefore, found it extremely fascinating from that point of view. I have turned the manuscript over to one of our medical school librarians who is acquainted with some of the editors at the University of Oklahoma Press. She plans to read the manuscript and then discuss it with the people at the O.U. Press. I will get back to you as soon as there is any word from them.

Sincerely,

[Signed]

Professor of Medicine

Several weeks after forwarding me his initial response, the medical professor called and informed me that the "O.U. Press decided to pass on *Gypsy*." He wished me luck with the manuscript. I wished him luck with kidney stone operations.

A number of small press editors and owners wrote me as a result of the *Publishers Weekly* article. In their letters they requested to see the manuscript (or excerpts from it), and they took occasional swipes at the publishing giants of New York. My experiences with Woodhix Press and *Albino*

*Cockroaches* were pleasant enough on a literary level, but a disaster on a financial one. *Albino* failed to make the press and me into millionaires, or "thousandaires" or "hundredaires," not even in Italian currency. So, I debated for a good while before responding to those typically friendly letters from the small press scene. Here is a sample written by the director-editor of a small press in the (201) Area Code, an editor for whom I instantly developed a sense of admiration and respect:

Dear Professor Hanna:

Without having read your book—but having read your article in *Publishers Weekly*—I am writing a fan letter. I like your book. That is to say, the essence, the concept, the inherent audacity, the immanent charm.

I offer a prophecy: somewhere in the outer precints of publishing—I refer to the small press legions—you will find a publisher for your book. It may even happen that this lead article in PW will galvanize some "big league" publisher.

Anyway, I want to read at least a portion of this manuscript that you have sent to so many of the establishment. How about the prologue, the epilogue, and the first chapter and the last chapter?

I close with a happy thought, a consolation, and a horror story. The happy thought is that the PW article reveals a gifted imagination, and will almost certainly bring valuable opportunities your way. The consolation is that happenstance, not justice, almost always governs the fate of the unknown writer these days. The horror story is that in the current economics of publishing one could have a solid book published and see it flow down the tubes and into the shredder.

A solid small press, devoted to quality, may indeed come your way and give your book long, satisfying, and eventually profitable life.

Best of luck to you. . . .

[Signed]

Editor

In the end, I decided against forwarding *The Gypsy Scholar* to this editor or to others on the small press circuit. I tried one final, perhaps weird, approach, but before mentioning it, I must refer to a disturbing editorial suggestion that came up on several occasions. The suggestion was outlined in detail by a director of a university press in New York state. Picking up on my one-time duties as a football coach in Kansas, the director responded by diagraming a game plan for publishing the manuscript. His letter stated:

Dear Coach Hanna:
Did you know that Mark Twain self-published many of his works? Neither did I, but, given the ping-pong response you have gotten from publishers on *The Gypsy Scholar*, that might not be a bad idea for you. They all seem to say that you write well, with humor, but someone else ought to publish your works. Maybe you should think about publishing it yourself.

Here's a plan of sorts, if you want to take the idea seriously:

About tax refund time next year get a few low-to-middle-income friends together (those most apt to receive a refund) and form a publishing corporation to do this book. You will need to raise about $6,000 to capitalize the corporation. Invite a banker or rich relative or two in if needs be. Find a typesetter to set the manuscript in type. That should be easy from your word-processed manuscript, and shouldn't cost more than $1,000. Arrange with a printer to print 2,000 copies in paperback (you, or someone, will have to design a paperback cover). That should cost about $2,500. Price the book at $9.95.

Now comes the hard part—selling the book. First, send about 50 copies, free, to review editors or reviewers of the major review media. That will leave you 1,950 copies to sell. Those will most likely go to wholesalers, library jobbers, libraries, bookstores, and individual buyers. The problem is to reach those folks with information about the book.

First, you will need a name for your publishing company. Flagship Press comes to mind. Next, you will need a mailing piece. You can, if you are computer-clever, have a good word processing program, and have a printer that can produce a few type fonts of letter-quality type, produce this yourself. (You could also produce camera ready copy of the book for your printer in this way if you have a lot of time and patience.) Finally, buy appropriate mailing lists and labels from the American Library Association, the American Bookseller's Association, the Educational Directory, the College Marketing Group, the National Association of College Stores, the Association of Gypsy Scholars, if there is one. (If not, there ought to be.)

Send your mailing piece 4 to 6 weeks before you are to receive bound books from your printer. Offer the following terms to your customers: 40% discount off list price on multiple orders (this will attract your jobbers, wholesalers, and bookstores); 20% to libraries; cash with orders for individual orders; that is, full list price plus $1.00 for postage and handling.

Pack your 1,950 new books in your garage or cellar and fill orders as they come in. If all goes well you will sell out the edition, pay off your corporate partners, and realize enough profit to finance a reprint if the market demand is still there, or pocket almost enough to pay you for your efforts if the demand for a reprint does not exist. If all does not go well you know what it is like, and may qualify, to be a university press publisher. At least you will have spent a lot of time not reading rejection letters.

Yours truly,

[Signed]

Director

The director did not know, however, that I detested vanity publishing far more than a beauty queen candidate detests a flourishing platoon of pimples. He, at least, recommended the do-it-yourself vanity formula; the let-them-do-it-for-cash vanity formula is the one that made my hair stand—on the sides of my head, that is. Rather than self-publish *The Gypsy Scholar*, I decided to try it on a few more publishers with a cover letter that used that old suicide one-liner that I had used with my curriculum vita in search of a teaching position. The letter read:

> Dear Editor or Director:
> [Addressed by name]
>     Might this interest you, or do you recommend literary
> suicide?
>
>                                   Sincerely,
>
>                                   S. S. HANNA
>
>                                   Department of English
>
> Enclosures

I sent the letter and the manuscript's extensive prospectus
to several commercial and university presses. Some de-
clined to see *The Gypsy Scholar*, others invited it, one even
suggested how it can be made "food for thought"; all referred to the word "suicide" in their responses. Here are
three typical responses:

> Dear Professor Hanna:
>     Although we can't publish your book—we're too small,
> too poor and committed for the next year or so to manu-
> scripts already under contract—I do not recommend lit-
> erary suicide.
>     I do recommend that you retain a literary agent (they
> are all listed in the Literary Market Place), for your book
> belongs with a largish publisher, and the only way you
> can get said publisher to look up from his tuna fish sand-
> wich is to have an agent shoving your ms. past the celery.
> If the manuscript is as entertaining and informative as
> your prospectus, you will get your book published.
>
> Best of luck.
>
> Sincerely,
>
> [Signed]
>
> Editor

Dear Mr. Hanna:

Suicide, at least as pronounced in these parts (s-e-p-p-u-k-u), is apt to be a bit messy. No doubt there is much more in store for the gypsy scholar—perhaps a chapter on trying to get the manuscript published?

If you get it all down, I hope you will credit us with prophesying that the manuscript will be published—perseverance furthers—but not by a press whose areas of interest are Asia and the Pacific.

Good hunting.

Sincerely,

[Signed]

Editor


Dear Professor Hanna:

Please don't invest in literary suicide, your imaginative spirit is much too important to dull-witted people like myself. I'd love to read whatever you've written, but I don't think that anybody here would be interested in publishing it, it's just not the kind of thing that we do. I'm going to be out of the office for a few weeks, so why not send a couple of chapters to my home at: _____ . What I wonder immediately from your outline is whether or not you ever thought of turning this into a novel, clearly so much of what you have to say will be taken more seriously if people don't see it as a personal self-centered memoir. Let me know if you agree.

Best regards,

[Signed]

Editor


Dictated by Mr. _____ and signed in his absence.


From my extensive attempts to publish *The Gypsy Scholar*—the first half of which was a record of my academic journey and the second, my spiritual pilgrimage—I learned many lessons. I learned, for example, how difficult it is to sell a book manuscript that is directed at a crossover audience of academicians and evangelicals. I learned that editors at commercial houses or university presses often give contradictory advice. I learned that commercial editors live in fear of their sales forces and the university presses dread their faculty committees. I learned that both kinds of publishers have extremely hard-working, helpful people who often exhibit strong, personal interest in unknown writers. I learned that one has to find a creative way to get past the "slush pile," and one of the best ways to do that is to forward the manuscript FIRST CLASS, to an editor or director by name, and to include a strange cover letter with it. I learned not to be cowed by rejection letters whether they came directly or via a literary agent. I learned to wait—and wait—for editorial responses. Above all, I learned to flavor my self-confidence as a struggling writer (and, for that matter, as a struggling professor) with a dash of self-deprecating humor.

While having lunch with four colleagues at a professional conference in Chicago, I applied one of the lessons that I had learned. In the course of a heated publish or perish discussion, one gentleman said, "Oh, you can get just about anything published these days." And to that I replied, "Most people who make that odd claim have no rejection letters or slips in their files and no published items on their vitas. Maybe what you want to say," I continued, with a touch of satisfaction in my voice, "is that you can have anything privately printed these days, but to have it professionally published is another matter." I reached for my cup of coffee and added, "After all that I had done in trying to market a book manuscript, I now feel that it's easier for a fingerless fellow to become a surgeon, a urologist, or even a prostate specialist than (for me at least) to publish a book."

After the conference, I drove up to Milwaukee to spend a few days with my parents, sisters, and in-laws. "When are you going to stop moving around from college to college?" my mother asked, as we ate breakfast in our modest house located in the inner city near Marquette University.

"When I get tenure somewhere."

"And when will that be?" she asked, as I admired the

deep furrows of her beautiful face.

"Who knows? It doesn't look promising now. I'm praying simply to hold on to the job that I now hold."

Once again, she trotted out my in-laws who in her mind had "made it." She spoke with pride of the First Wisconsin National Bank and Johnsons Controls where they work, and I spoke with pride about Geneva College. At that breakfast I made a mistake in telling her about *The Gypsy Scholar* and about all the problems that I had in trying to get it published. "You'll never see me on the 'Today' show talking about it," I said.

"But how do all these other people get their books published?" she asked.

"Frankly, I don't know."

"What are you going to do with it now?"

"My latest idea is to shorten *The Gypsy Scholar* and add to it a few sections on all the problems—and, oh yes, fun— that I had in trying to get it published."

"If it's like that cockroach book, I can see why you had problems with it."

"No, Mother, this is prose; the cockroaches were poems."

"And you say you tried?"

"Believe me, Mother, I've tried."

# *Afterword*
## *Dropping Anchor*
## *at the Other Geneva*

Frustrations and failure breed a certain wit, one that often appears more entertaining in hindsight. As it turned out, I survived the faculty "cuts" enacted during my first year at Geneva College. While teaching, I continued the search for a book publisher. In time, I received two contracts: one for academic tenure at Geneva and the other for the publication of this book, an abridged version of *The Gypsy Scholar* and the correspondence that the unabridged version had generated. My relentless pursuit of both contracts must have resembled that of a seasoned but hard-headed scholar searching for the mother of the Unknown Soldier.

Tenure deepened my interest in Geneva. It led me to offer several ideas to the college's president, and I offered those ideas via memos. Here is the content of one memo:

> A while back, I mentioned to you an idea for a mascot. I thought a bit more about that idea, and I'm now detailing my thoughts for whatever they're worth.
> The idea is a simple one: You might wish to consider assigning to our "hot shot" engineers a project that would

consist of attaching a ribbon/ribbons to the center of a frisbee; the feat would be to design a frisbee-ribbon that when properly launched would create a tornadolike pattern.

The frisbee-ribbon could combine the school's colors; it could be sold at concession booths or thrown into the stands after touchdowns; cheerleaders could fling it around the gym during basketball time-outs, to mention a few of the possibilities. All sorts of data could be printed on the frisbee and the ribbon. Such data might include a few words on the history of the college, its strong programs, majors offered, Latin motto, a sketch of Old Main, athletic records, and so forth. The mascot's name might well be: Flying Colors.

Most importantly, in an era when many colleges are competing for students, the frisbee-ribbon could be mass produced and included in packets to potential students. High school students these days receive all sorts of printed items in the mail; the items create a colossal pile of excellence-ego froth (whatever that means). In any event, all those items tend to look alike.

The question that we might well be asking is this: What should we do to isolate Geneva's data from the pile? The answer, of course, is to accompany our data with an award winning frisbee—a frisbee with a ribbon. The frisbee is such an unusual idea that potential students and their parents will remember it, tell their neighbors and friends about it, play with it, joke about it, and—when they sober up, as it were—act on it.

A frisbee might well help us make the education sections of *Time* and *Newsweek*, especially on stories that refer to creative ways to call attention to the college's programs. And since our nickname is the Golden Tornadoes, the idea will appear to be less of a gimmick and more of a creative way to exploit our name. It might also make the *Chronicle of Higher Education*. Indeed, the frisbee might even be used in a full-page ad in *Campus Life*. The finest ad in that magazine is done by Judson College, and the ad uses balloons.

These are quick thoughts that come to mind. I'm sure other thoughts could be grafted on this basic idea. An unrelated idea that I have deals with that big vacant slab of wall above the entrance to Clarke Hall, the wall that faces the heart of the campus. Wouldn't a large, spectacular, controversial (i.e. modern) metal sculpture look good there?

A second memo that I had written and planned to forward to the Geneva College president outlined a magazine ad that featued the slogan "The Other Geneva." I felt that the slogan might be a timely one since Geneva—thanks to the arms talks—often made the national and international news and was likely to do so for years to come. The slogan's drawback (one that I refused to mention in the memo) was in the European Geneva's association with cuckoo clocks.

A third memo dealt with a plan that had me training a young lady to kick an extra point in the traditional Oberlin-Geneva football game. The kick, as I envisioned it, would serve a three-fold purpose: bring the college free national publicity, enter the college's name in American sports history, and call attention, not only to Geneva's established programs in women's athletics such as tennis, softball, basketball, and volleyball, but also to its brand new program in varsity soccer, a program that I coached.

It is difficult to predict the response of the Geneva College president to all these ideas. Suffice it to say, I loved his positive response to my candidacy for tenure status with the Golden Tornadoes.

Norm Podhoretz wrote an engaging autobiographic book and entitled it *Making It*. In his profession, Mr. Podhoretz's achievements rank him among the "few," the famous, the phenomenal. My achievements, by contrast, place me among the "many" who discover that genetic and environmental factors often prevent us from making it big in our chosen professions.

Like most who fail to make it big, I refuse to surrender to suicide. Instead, I invest in a sense of humor and go on "hacking it," doing my best to survive and achieve. In so doing, my life reflects that of (almost) Everyman.

My rejection letters might also reflect those of every writer. My wife pirated a special letter from the file cabinet, had it professionally framed, and gave it to me as a present on the Christmas before I had received the contract for this book. The letter, written in response to the prospectus and the early parts of *The Gypsy Scholar*, carried a crest with the Latin word for "truth" divided into a triangular pattern: the "VE" and the "RI" were positioned at the top, and the "TAS" at the bottom—all were placed on open books.

The letter alluded to the early parts of *The Gypsy Scholar* and attempted to resonate with their humor. Signed by a member from the editorial department at the Harvard University Press, the entire letter stated:

Dear S. S.:

First off, congratulations in Beaver Falls. And how thick was the envelope that brought that news? Or was it a phone call?

I'm curious as to why you sent a Behavioral Sciences editor, Eric Wanner, material from your very funny manuscript, *The Gypsy Scholar*. No doubt there's cognitive something in there somewhere, but it would seem a Social Science editor might have been more appropriate, that is if you're bent on having the book published as nonfiction.

Anyway, it was given to me with a note that read: "Please decline—but read it first; it's wonderful." So now amid the mountains of rejection letters screaming for my attention, I've got to write one to a man that analyzes them for a living. Thanks, pal. ("What if he suspects I didn't use real stationery? Will he continue to read after he realizes I'm not going to ask for the manuscript? Is my signature going to end up as bathroom wallpaper?")

Some unsolicited advice for an unsolicited proposal: You're missing the subway, S. S. You obviously are able to tell a captivating story while turning some funny phrases. Why not hop on the autobiographical fiction genre bandwagon, get yourself an agent in New York that goes to lunch a lot, and put *Gypsy* on the *Fiction* map. Aren't you the least bit seduced by any of the constraints that

fiction would remove from your writings?
  Good luck, sport.

Truly yours,

[Signed]

Editorial Department

The Harvard editor offered earnest advice that I had already explored. Throughout my search for a publisher, I never gave up on *The Gypsy Scholar;* I often reworked segments of it, and in this final version, I preserved the academic journey, submerged the spiritual one, and narrated many of the letters that I had sent and received on the manuscript.

Oklahoma Baptist University, a solid school when I was there, continues to be a strong academic institution. Sterling College now is better than ever, thanks to new leadership and a steady increase in enrollment. And Geneva, America's Geneva, marches on with renewed vigor.

Someday—if the good folks in Oklahoma or Kansas would consider having me back—I would love to return and teach English in Shawnee or coach football on the prairies. But I would hate to try to market another nonfiction, autobiographical book manuscript, not unless my fortunes become so sensational that I find it impossible to keep them out of the *National Enquirer.*